OTHER WORKS
by
BENJAMIN WALLACE

NOVELS

Post-Apocalyptic Nomadic Warriors:
A Duck & Cover Adventure

Tortugas Rising

Horror in Honduras
(The Bulletproof Adventures of Damian Stockwell)

MORE DUMB WHITE HUSBAND

The Big Book of Dumb White Husband

NON-FICTION

Giving The Bird: The Indie Author's Guide to Twitter

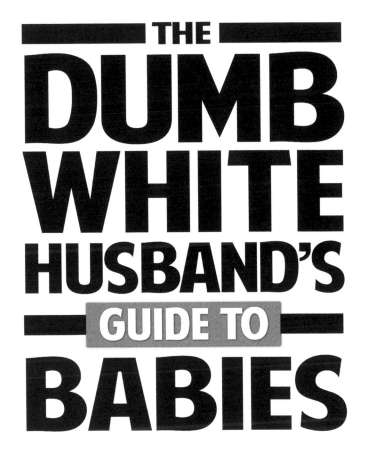

THE DUMB WHITE HUSBAND'S GUIDE TO BABIES

By Benjamin Wallace

ISBN-13: 978-1479305612
ISBN-10: 1479305618

This book is for entertainment purposes only. While every caution has been taken to provide readers with the most accurate information, readers are using the information in this book at their own risk. It is, after all, called The Dumb White Husband's Guide to Babies.

Cover design by MonkeyPAWcreative.

For every guy that always
longed to bring a child into this world
or forgot to pull out.

ABOUT THIS GUIDE

A lot of things change when your wife has a baby. You've probably heard something like that already. You've talked to friends and family. Many people have offered, or will offer, unsolicited advice. You may have even read some books about what it's going to be like to be a father.

Well guess what. They're lying to you.

Okay, "lying" may be stretching things a bit. But, they certainly aren't telling you everything. Why? Because having a child is exactly like buying a motorcycle.

When you are shopping for a motorcycle everyone tells you how cool it's going to be. When you buy a motorcycle, the same people tell you every gruesome accident story they've ever heard.

When you're having a kid, everyone tells you how wonderful it's going to be. They tell you how your heart will melt the first time they call you "Dada." They tell you when your child will learn to walk. They tell you when to switch from baby food to solids. They never tell you that one day your kid may habitually take his shit and rub it in his hair.

Lucky for you, you've got me.

I've got no training, no degree and almost no social skills. But I do have three kids—two boys and a girl. They're awesome. And they've each driven me to the brink of insanity well before they could speak. But, I've survived and you might too.

I'm certainly not trying to talk anyone out of having kids. They're wonderful. Really. The happiness my three kids bring me far outweighs the frustration, so don't take any of this the wrong way. They are a complete joy.

Besides, if you've picked up this book you've probably already got a little screaming miracle at home or on the way. So, you're already in.

A lot of ground has been covered in the impending baby category and they are all full of great knowledge about what's happening to your baby and your wife at various stages. I'll cover some of that here, but I'm really trying to tell you the things that those books, family and professionals won't.

At times you will feel like a terrible parent. At other times you'll feel like a champion. Most times, you'll feel like an idiot. That's all completely normal, you just need to know it's coming.

Just consider this whole guide thing a "heads up" or a "watch out" or a "hey, you're kid might put crap in his hair, just thought you should know" kind of thing. I know it would have been a comfort for me to know that all the things my wife and I went through were completely normal and not the result of some poor parenting skills.

There's a whole bunch of stuff you're not expecting when your wife is expecting. I'm just trying to share what I know. Besides, I've picked up some tricks that might help.

TERMS

I promise not to get all scientific-jargony on you. That would just confuse us both. But, I do want to clarify a couple of choices I've made in writing this book regarding some of the terms.

Wife

I'm not naïve or a prude in any way. I understand that you may be having a child with someone who is not your wife. For simplicity sake, however, I'll be referring to the person who is carrying your child as your wife.

If that is not the case, when you get to the word wife, just mentally replace it with girlfriend, mistress, acquaintance, or disgraced cousin—whatever the case may be.

He/She/It

If you don't know what kind of kid your having, how would I know? I'm going to try and stick with gender-neutral terms but if I slip and say she and you end up having a he, know that a he is just like a she but with more penis.

THE TWIN VERSION

Throughout this guide you'll find sections called THE TWIN VERSION. I went from one kid to three in the span of two minutes so I understand the added challenges that come with multiples. In "the twin version" sections I'll explain how having multiples changes things. It usually makes things trickier but I'll also show how to milk this situation for all of the sympathy it's worth. The more children you have at the same time, the more pity you get. Let's not waste it.

THE FIRST THING NO ONE TOLD YOU

You're going to have to change the kitty litter, man. I know how you feel. This would have been the one deal breaker for me too, but no one told us that a woman with child could not be around kitty litter until after my wife was pregnant.

I realize that this sounds like something women made up to get out of changing the litter, but the fact is that cat poop and even kitty litter dust contains a chemical that could cause Toxoplasmosis. And you know that's bad because the word starts with toxo, which is Latin for "this shit'll kill your baby."

You'd think that with such a potentially lethal effect that all kitty litter bags should be marked with a skull and crossbones and that cats would be outlawed as pets. Despite my letter writing campaign, neither is the case. We're just going to have to live with the evil creatures. Just know that the bag of dirt with the cute kitten on it is in fact a chemical weapon designed to end your family line.

Kitty litter is only the first way that your wife's cat will try to murder your offspring. We'll get to that a little later. Just remember that cat = baby death. Got it?

And, before you ask, I already checked—even with a surgical mask, the litter is dangerous, so you're going to have to change her cat's litter for the next nine months. There's no use whining about it, just dig in. Sorry, man.

FINDING OUT

With the exception of conception, every part of childbirth is disgusting. I'm not just talking about the natural and gross biology parts. We ingenious humans have gone and made things worse through technology.

Let's take for instance the very first time you find out that you're going to be a father. You're going to have the admirable job of raising a young man or woman up into the world. Your influence, guidance and love are certain to produce a fine upstanding citizen that will go on to accomplish great things. He or she could even be president of a great nation one day.

How do you find out about this blessing? What is your first awareness of this joy of joys? Your wife waves a stick in your face that she spent the morning peeing all over.

Although it is the most effective way to detect early pregnancy, this method is hardly the most dignified. Then again, it might be the best way to kick off the next poop- and pee-filled years. As you are about to be a parent, this will hardly be your last experience with bodily fluids. Maybe it is secretly meant as a coronation to don up on you your new title as if there is some silent authority declaring, "With the scepter of urine I do declare you father-to-be. Now rise and take the pee stick."

If this hasn't already happened, the only advice I can really offer is this—if she hands the stick to you, grab it from the end she is holding. She knows what she did to that thing and where exactly it had to be done.

How you react at this moment is a good indicator to her how you will be as a father. Oddly enough, saying nothing is appropriate. Stammering for words is an expected and endearing reaction. Swearing, downing a bottle of Jack or changing your name and moving to Mexico are less acceptable reactions.

No matter how you choose to react, don't forget to hug her. Just make sure she's put the pee stick down first.

YOUR DUE DATE

Admittedly, the pee stick is a pretty exciting moment. The two of you will grin for hours. All eye contact will result in goofy smiles. Enjoy that moment because it is the last one that does not also include the doctor. Once the magic whiz wand says you're expecting, it's off to the doctors to make everything official. The test is essentially the same but the doctor will require a lot more pee and fewer sticks. They are looking for a hormone. Let them handle this one. They'll find the hormone and give you the good news—your wife did not waste ten bucks peeing on a stick.

Once they confirm that your wife is indeed pregnant, the next step is to determine your baby's due date. There's a chance you may know the exact date of conception. And you can tell the doctor. But they don't care and they won't listen. As far as modern medical science is concerned, every single couple did it the day after the wife's last cycle. Apparently, in medical school, they learn that it is the only day that people have sex. Even if you have photographic evidence of the exact time and date of conception, you pervert. It doesn't matter to them. The first day after the last period is the day your child was conceived.

So what do they do with this information? Do they enter it into the computer where a complex algorithm calculates a due date based on biological, geographical and socio-economical information? No. They pull out a decoder wheel. They line up the date the doctor has decided that you had sex and it gives them a date forty weeks in the future and that's your due date.

From this point on nearly every conversation you have will revolve around that date. Every deadline you now face will be determined by it. It is the end all, be all date. And, the chances of your baby getting there on that actual day are round about zero.

But, that's the date. Just go with it.

NINE MONTHS

A quick note about nine months; it's really ten. Yeah, I know, it's the one thing you thought you knew about having a baby. You knew how they were made and, once you were done with that part, you knew that nine months later you would have a baby.

The gestational term for human babies is forty weeks. That's ten months—even if February is doing something weird that year.

So why do British actors insist on telling us it's nine months? Well, usually by the time you find out you're wife is pregnant it's already been a month. So ten minus that one is nine. Simple math really. But, it stills seems like a cruel trick from across the pond.

So how will this affect things? Not at all really. I just wanted you to know so you don't look like an idiot arguing with the doctor when she tries to tell you a baby is full term at ten months and you keep going, "nuh-uh, it's nine."

WHEN TO TELL
THE WORLD

For a whole lot of reasons, you're probably going to want to tell the world that you got a woman pregnant. So, how long do you wait? Traditionally, people advise that you wait about three months before announcing the pregnancy. Unfortunately, many pregnancies end in a miscarriage before this time and the advice is based on not letting the cat out of the bag before the baby is out of the woods.

Go ahead. Try and wait three months without the world getting wind of this. You or your wife will slip eventually. Probably sooner than later. Perhaps you'll just agree to tell your parents with the caveat that they don't tell anybody else. Sure, that'll work. You don't think grandma-to-be is going to tell everybody she knows? Of course, she'll also add the caveat that they don't tell anybody, too. Grandmas are wily that way.

No matter what you decide, the world will know soon enough. Maybe it just picks up on the look on your face that is either overly joyous or absent of all color. It all depends on how hard you were actually trying to have a baby.

Regardless of what you decided, people will be excited for you and your wife. Your mothers will cry, her friends will squeal and jaded fathers will pretend you've ruined everything. It's inevitable. Just shake all the hands, five all the highs and get ready to hear all about the fucking milkman.

THE FUCKING MILKMAN

After you've decided to let everyone know the wonderful news, you'll receive a host of compliments, well wishes and assaults on your wife's virtue. The most common of these is an insistence that the milkman is actually the father of your child.

I cannot tell you why guys find this funny. There is no other good news in this world that is greeted with an accusation of a spouse's sluttery. There's no other situation where it happens.

You: "Hey, I got that new job."
Guy: "That's great. Bet your wife boned your new boss."
Or
You: "We close on the house next week."
Guy: "I guess your wife is sleeping with the agent."
Or
You: "Good news. I don't have cancer after all."
Guy: "Your wife's a whore."

See? It's never really appropriate. But, as soon as you say you're having a kid, some guy will insist your wife screwed the milkman.

This is insulting for two reasons: one, it implies that the love of your life and mother of your child-to-be has been unfaithful; two, it implies that she has invented a time machine and used it to travel sixty years into the past to have a dalliance in the dairy industry rather than use it to prevent the B-52s from forming as any responsible human would.

It's inevitable, however, so you're just going to have to deal with it. And, since throat punching unoriginal, unfunny coworkers is still "frowned upon" by most HR departments, the best you can do is smile and remind the person that it is the 21st century and that milk has not been delivered to a home in over fifty years due to advances in refrigeration, packaging and the fact that all the milkmen are still over at his mom's house taking turns making deliveries at her back door. (Guys that make milkman jokes really like your mom jokes, too, so they should find the mental image of a line of geriatric deliverymen banging their mother in the pooper hysterical). Don't forget to smile. It's all in good fun.

THE RIGHT TO COMPLAIN

The moment you're wife tells you she's pregnant, you lose the right to complain. You'll get it back eventually but any grumblings you have for the next nine months to three years should be kept to yourself.

That's not to say that you won't have things to complain about. Over the course of her pregnancy you'll be doing the bulk of the work and the deeper into it she gets, the heavier things seem to get.

You'll have to lift everything. You'll have to assemble everything that a kid needs. You'll even be expected to paint a mural. Maybe you have mural painting skills already. Perhaps you're known throughout the land as an excellent muralist. Maybe it's been your lifelong dream to quit your job and paint vistas on old brick walls or the beds of pickup trucks. Or maybe the only thing you ever painted was that crappy five-fingered turkey in second grade. No matter your muralist experience, you'll be expected to execute some artistic work on the wall of a nursery that will stir the imagination of a child without giving it nightmares. It will be elaborate. There may be squirrels. And you'll have no doubt that you can't pull it off. But you will have to try and then fail. All without complaining.

Lifting things and painting murals isn't the half of it. There's plenty of crap to do around the house and even more to do outside of it. And the shopping. Holy crap, the shopping. This baby hasn't even developed eyes yet and it already has more clothes than you. And, some of them are already being returned. There's going to be a ton of parties that you have to go to. And there's a doctor's appointment about every two to three minutes. Between all of this and the rest of it, there is absolutely no one back at the house painting the damn mural. And those squirrels aren't going to paint themselves.

But, you don't get to complain.

I don't care if you're feeling neglected, had a bad day at work or been shot in the ass with an errant crossbow bolt. If you say anything, it will be considered insensitive. She's having your baby. She's sacrificing her body to bring life into this world and you're bitching about being shot? What's wrong with you?

I'm assuming you already knew this and planned to keep

quiet, but I just thought I'd mention it just in case. After all, you've somehow put yourself in a situation where you got shot with a crossbow so you've already demonstrated poor decision making skills. I thought the reminder couldn't hurt.

YOUR FIRST SONOGRAM

This is where the magic becomes real. This is where all theories are confirmed, all doubts are removed and you will no longer be able to fool yourself into thinking that maybe your wife is just getting fat. You'll hear heartbeats and you'll see cell growth all through the magic of television. Your friend, television.

The machine is really quite amazing. Your wife will be asked to lift up her shirt, they'll squirt sonogram helping liquid on her belly and wave a little device that looks something like a CB receiver across her cute and growing tummy until they find little baby you in there. The technician will take some measurements and let you listen to the heartbeat. Don't worry, it's supposed to sound exactly like you swishing mouthwash around.

They'll even print you out a picture—the first ever picture of your baby. Your wife will show it to family, friends and anyone willing to listen. And, you'll look at the picture and you'll …

Look, it's important here that you at least pretend to see what everyone is talking about in the picture. You may not have a clue to what is in the grainy little photo—just fake it. It's easier for everyone. Besides, you'll have more sonograms along the way. In later trips, the baby will even look like a baby. This magic screen will even tell you what kind of baby you're having. There is nothing TV can't do.

One last thing: if they don't use the wand, don't ask about the wand. Just pretend it isn't there. Ignore the wand.

THE TWIN VERSION
a.k.a. The Scariest Thing I've Ever Seen on TV

When you go in for your first sonogram, the last thing you're expecting is to discover that you are so awesome you were able to knock up your wife twice with just one try. But being awesome and being prepared for shocking news are two different things. Here's what happened when we had our sonogram:

The woman with the wand didn't see it. (Don't ask about

the wand). My wife had suffered a miscarriage a few months before. So when the sonogram tech saw my son, she zoomed in to assure us that every thing was okay.

She measured everything she could at that age and turned to enter the information. The wand moved.

"What's that? That's not ..."

She turned back to the screen.

"That's a kidney, right, I mean it's her bladder or something." It was small and bean shaped. I knew that kidneys were bean shaped.

"Oh, we have twins."

The miscarriage had resulted in a rush to the hospital and a quick surgery. So naturally we had really hoped that everything would be fine with this early sonogram. Apparently we had hoped really hard.

We were both shocked. We both just kept saying "twins" to each other over and over and smiling out of fear, excitement and fear.

Once the panic stops, the first step is to assign blame. Start with family histories and work your way down to the individual. We had fraternal twins so we knew that it was not my fault. I'm not the one that went dropping two eggs. Once blame has been assigned, you move on to the third step, which is resume panicking. This lasts a while.

The shock lasted weeks. It was only then that we could say it without laughing nervously. It was our own fault. We had walked in to having a second child thinking we had it all figured out. We knew what we really needed to get from the baby store and what was bull. We had a crib and a swing. We were covered. We were wrong.

We had gotten cocky. And now we had to pay for it.

It's difficult to explain what it's like finding out that you're having twins. You get that panic coldness in your stomach like when you get caught doing something wrong and there is no one else around to blame. It is such an unbelievable moment that you begin to question all of reality. Even gravity seems affected as everything seems to float. You can't even do math anymore as any attempt is now doubled. People speak to you, but you don't hear them. You just nod along.

Simply put, you're terrified. And you're right to be.

YOU BECOME NOBODY

Something else happens during the sonogram that may not be as evident. Once that child is visible on the screen, you cease to exist. It's not a slow fade like your existence has been undone due to some tampering with the space-time continuum; it's very sudden. The doctor will know it. Your wife will know it. Recent studies show that the fetus, which is only a few cells at this point, knows it. It just may not be very evident to you.

You'll try to speak and no one will hear you. You'll have thoughts and no one will care. If you start to mess with the equipment in the room, like say picking up the sonogram wand and making ray gun noises, they will notice and tell you to quit. But as soon as you put the wand down, you'll go back to not existing.

It's nothing you did. The doctor's primary concern from here on out is your wife and baby's safety and health. Your wife's concern is for the baby. You've done your part. And, as far as making a baby goes, it's out of your hands at this point.

You will start to notice your new non-role slowly. Your wife and the doctor will begin to talk in a language that you don't understand. You'll notice that they never really turn to you anymore. No one will ask how you're feeling. No one cares if you've been eating right. No one cares if you're doing your Kegels.

It's okay, really. Let the code-talkers have their secret language. All you have to do is be supportive and nod when you think it's expected. If you've been married for any length of time, this should be second nature by now anyway.

FINE, ABOUT THE WAND

There's two ways the sonogram tech can make the magic TV show you your baby. The first, as I said, is to squirt some jelly on your wife's belly and move what looks like a circa 1972 Radio Shack mouse over it.

Sometimes the baby is harder to find. Sometimes a closer look is needed. So they grab the wand and "lift up your shirt" becomes "take off your pants." They slip a condom over the thing and in they go to look for the baby. They don't even have a fancy term for the condom so you can't even pretend it's something else. It would be easier if it was called a latex barrier or wand cover or a Wankle sock or something. Any of these would be better. But, no, they're individually wrapped and come together on a strip.

This is also when you become very aware whether your wife's doctor is a man or a woman. I'm not saying you didn't notice before, I'm just saying that at that moment there is a voice in the back of your head that is saying, "that dude/chick just ..."

The important thing is don't forget to smile. This is still a "special moment" no matter what's up your wife.

Told you not to ask about the wand. Kind of wishing you hadn't picked it up and made ray gun noises now, aren't you?

THE ADVANCED SONOGRAM

The advancements that have been made in modern medicine are amazing. And while most of them are used for good instead of evil, there is also the 3D sonogram. This horrific upgrade is usually optional and costs extra.

I'm no doctor. I don't know if the image is helpful to the baby doctor, but I do know this: the people with the machine will try to sell you on it by telling you that you will get a picture of what your baby really looks like. You'll see facial features, ears, eyes etcetera ...

Imagine, a real picture of how your pride and joy will actually look. How could you resist?

Resist. Don't do it. Please don't do it. Because you'll think you're baby is going to look just like a Garbage Pail Kid. I've never seen one 3D sonogram that didn't give me nightmares. You'll see it that way too. But you won't be able to admit it. You just spent money on this thing and you were told that the lumpy clay-looking monstrosity is what your child will look like. You'll hold it up proudly and creep people out and force them to lie and say it's cute too.

You'll know that they're lying and deep down you'll be afraid of the image, too. You should fear the birth of your child but only because of the crushing weight of being responsible for the life of another human being. Not because you think it's going to look like Sloth from *The Goonies*.

Look, do it if you must but don't expose others to it. And, if you have done it already, rest assured your son or daughter will look nothing like Stabby Abbie or Puke Luke when it emerges. Not at all. It will be much more gross than that. If I had to give the look a name, I'd go with After Bertha.

THE BABY CLASS

Baby class is nothing at all like what we saw on sitcoms. It's way longer and you learn about way more than how to tell your wife to breathe.

The baby class is a great place to learn about babies. In fact, you'll learn so much about how to clean, test water for, rock, hold and feed babies, that you won't remember one bit of it. A lot of information will be flying at you, but this is the only thing you need to get—how to swaddle a baby. Some call it the baby burrito. I don't care what you call it, that shit will save your sanity. Pay attention to that and you'll be okay.

Aside from swaddling, there are a couple of other things you'll learn in baby class. First of all, cats will try to murder your baby. It's true. They asked who had dogs; my wife and I raised our hands. The baby teacher said that was great; dogs are very protective of the baby and may even sleep underneath the crib to stay close and guard them.

Then she asked who had cats. My wife raised her hand; I pointed to my wife. The baby teacher said those with cats would have to be really careful because cats are attracted to the soft breath of an infant and will climb into the crib and smother them. To death. Until they die. (If you can spin it, this is probably the best time to try for a cat free home—bonus, you won't have to change the litter anymore.) If you could possibly need any more proof that cats are evil, just look into their eyes. You see that look they have? They're not looking at you with admiration. They're wondering what your eyes taste like.

After they expose the evil nature of cats, the folks at the baby class make you watch a video to prepare you for being in the delivery room. I asked them, since it was supposed to be like in the delivery room, why not turn the TV around and hang up a sheet? The baby teacher smiled. I thought it was because she thought it was funny. It was because she knew something that they don't tell you. There is no sheet!

TV and movies have lied to us again. There is not some pristine blue sheet draped between you and the graphic and vicious act that is childbirth. You'll see everything. Everything!

So you have to watch the video. First off, no woman has been filmed giving birth since 1974. There's one video in the world and you're going to watch it. If it sounds terrible, don't worry. You probably already watched it in high school. You remember? They showed you the miracle of life and the only question anyone could think to ask was, "Why is it so hairy?" Yep, it's that same gal. Educating/grossing folks out since public school.

You'll leave the class with a touch of knowledge, a free diaper bag and a crap-ton of coupons that you'll never use.

But, you were there and you were supportive and that's what really matters.

THE TWIN VERSION

They'll tell you to take the Baby Class for Multiples. They'll tell you it's different than the regular baby class. The hospital gets paid for both. How different do you think it really is?

I'll tell you. It's not different at all. There are no secret juggling techniques. There are no magic tricks. The don't even tell you how to craft a medallion that you can split between two identical twins just in case they're separated and must later find one another to end a family curse.

Here's what you learn after wasting a day in the class—you got two babies instead of one. That's it.

Make sure you learn how to swaddle and practice not doing anything ever again. Here's your diploma.

SHOPPING: YOUR FIRST BABY FIGHT

When you leave the baby class you'll get a shopping checklist for newborns.

Your first fight will occur in Babies R Us, somewhere between the baby proofing section and the diaper rags. (Not the diapers. The diaper rags. Big difference. There is no sound reasoning behind the similar names.)

This fight will not be your fault. It won't be hers. And, there is no way around it. You will fight. And, you will most likely leave the store with nothing and be forced to come back and shop again. All you can do is blame the list that you'll see on the next page.

We already established that we don't know jack going into

this baby thing. Honestly, did you know that cats were fur-bearing murder machines made of an evil so foul that even their shit carried fetus-killing poison? Of course not. We always assumed, but we never knew for certain. So, how are we really supposed to react to this:

NURSERY
- crib
- crib mattress
- changing table
- glider & ottoman
- dressers
- chests & night stands
- armoires
- crib mobile
- wall border/decals
- diaper stackers
- nursery lighting
- window treatments
- closet organization
- storage baskets/pails

BEDDING
- crib bedding set
- fitted crib sheets
- mattress pads & covers
- swaddle & receiving blankets
- bassinet
- bassinet bedding
- sleep wedges & aids

CAR SEATS
- infant car seat
- convertible car seat
- booster car seat
- car seat bases
- car seat head supports
- car seats toys
- car seat savers
- car seat sun shades & mirrors
- car seat buntings & footmuffs

FEEDING
- breast pump
- breast milk storage
- nursing covers
- nursing pillow & stool
- infant positioner
- bottles
- nipples
- bibs
- burp cloths
- pacifiers
- bottle warmers & sterilizers
- bottle accessories
- dishes & bowls
- utensils
- high chair

STROLLER
- travel system stroller
- full-size stroller
- lightweight stroller
- jogging stroller
- double and triple stroller
- stroller buntings & footmuffs
- covers & shades
- organizers & holders
- stroller toys

DIAPERING
- diapers- up to 8 lbs
- diapers- 8 to 14 lbs
- baby wipes
- diaper bag
- baby changing pads & covers
- diaper creams & ointments
- diaper pails & refills

- wipe warmers dispensers
- portable changing pads & sets
- 2-4 spare diapers (if using cloth, add wraps or pins/covers)
- baby wipes (place refill wipes in travel case)
- changing pad (several if using disposables)
- diaper cream
- antibacterial gel/wipes
- plastic sealable bags for used diapers/dirty clothes
- 1-2 changes of clothes for baby
- formula (if not nursing)
- bottles (if not nursing)
- bibs & burp cloths
- breastfeeding wrap (if nursing)
- pacifier & pacifier case

PLAY TIME

- baby swing
- bouncer
- play yard
- 2-3 play yard sheets
- gym & play mat
- baby toys
- walker & jumper
- stationary entertainer
- books
- DVDs
- music
- early development toys
- interactive toys
- riding toys

CLOTHING

- bodysuits
- one pieces
- gowns
- socks
- hats
- wearable blankets
- gift sets
- matching sets
- baby shoes

BATHING

- bathtub
- 6-8 towels
- shampoo & body wash
- baby lotions & moisturizers
- grooming kits (brush, nail clippers)
- bath accessories
- bath toys
- washcloths
- bath robes
- dental care

SAFETY

- monitor
- thermometer
- first aid kit
- humidifier
- purifier
- gates
- outlet covers & plugs
- cabinet locks & straps
- car & travel safety
- kitchen & bath safety
- fire & home safety
- home first-aid kit
- aspirators

2 pages actually. Sorry.

That is the shopping list you're handed. It is so overwhelming that you have little choice but to trust it. After all, no one would try and bilk you when you're having a baby, right?

And what kind of parent would you be if you didn't get the best of every item? Don't you want the best for your child? Don't you want them to be safe? Don't you love them?

Of course you do. You must need absolutely everything on that list.

You'll go through the store and start filling up the cart. You'll think nothing of it at first, but the part of your brain that wasn't asleep during math class will eventually start to scream at you. With every new thing you put in the cart, the pit in your stomach/wallet will grow. You'll start to wonder if you really need all that stuff and even though you know nothing, you'll begin to figure out what you don't need. You'll start to voice your opinion and this is where the argument will start.

Frustration will build as you try to grapple with the different items, their purpose and their cost. The swearing will probably start when you find out that there are diapers (for butts) and diaper rags (for faces) and you begin to scream to no one that they shouldn't be given such similar names. The entire situation will collapse when you start looking at that thing that keeps the toilet seat locked down. You swear louder and storm out together leaving behind a cart full of baby crap, doomed to repeat the process because you're really going to need that crap.

Again, it's no one's fault. Your wife doesn't understand this anymore than you do. And there is no one involved with the list that doesn't have a vested interest in you buying everything on it.

Here's the real list:

NURSERY

- crib
- crib mattress
- ~~changing table~~ *floor*
- ~~glider & ottoman~~
- dresser~~s~~
- ~~chests & night stands~~ *really?*
- ~~armoires~~
- crib mobile
- ~~wall border/decals~~ *crappy mural*
- ~~diaper stackers~~ *boxes*
- ~~nursery~~ lighting
- ~~window treatments~~
- ~~closet organization~~
- storage baskets/pails

BEDDING

- crib bedding set
- fitted crib sheets
- mattress pads & covers
- *Yes!* → swaddle & receiving blankets
- ~~bassinet~~ *see crib*
- ~~bassinet bedding~~
- sleep wedges & aids

CAR SEATS

- infant car seat
- ~~convertible car seat~~ *do you own a convertible*
- booster car seat
- car seat bases
- car seat head supports
- car seats toys
- ~~car seat covers~~
- car seat sun shades & mirrors
- car seat ~~buntings~~ & ~~footmuffs~~

FEEDING

- ~~breast pump~~ *rent*
- breast milk storage
- nursing covers
- nursing pillow & stool
- infant positioner
- bottles
- nipples
- bibs
- burp cloths
- pacifiers
- bottle warmers & sterilizers
- bottle accessories
- dishes & bowls
- utensils
- high chair

STROLLER

- travel system stroller ⎤
- full-size stroller ⎟ *pick one*
- lightweight stroller ⎦
- jogging stroller
- double and triple stroller
- ~~stroller buntings & footmuffs~~
- covers & shades
- organizers & holders
- stroller toys

DIAPERING

- diapers- up to 8 lbs ⎤ *wait*
- diapers- 8 to 14 lbs ⎦
- baby wipes
- diaper bag
- baby changing pads & covers
- diaper creams & ointments
- ~~diaper pails & refills~~ *Trash can with a lid*

- ~~wipe warmers dispensers~~ *just don't refrigerate*
- portable changing pads & sets
- 2-4 spare diapers (if using cloth, add wraps or pins/covers)
- baby wipes (place refill wipes in travel case)
- changing pad (~~several if using disposables~~)
- diaper cream
- antibacterial gel/wipes
- ~~plastic sealable bags for used diapers/dirty clothes~~ *plastic bag*
- 1-2 changes of clothes for baby
- formula (if not nursing)
- bottles (if not nursing)
- bibs & burp cloths
- breastfeeding wrap (if nursing)
- pacifier & pacifier case

PLAY TIME

- baby swing
- bouncer
- ~~play yard~~ *use your yard*
- ~~2-3 play yard sheets~~
- gym & play mat
- baby toys
- walker & jumper
- stationary entertainer
- ~~books~~ *can't read*
- ~~DVDs~~ *can't see*
- music
- early development toys
- interactive toys
- ~~riding toys~~ *can't ride*

These are the same toys

CLOTHING

- bodysuits
- one pieces
- gowns *girls only*
- socks
- hats
- wearable blankets
- ~~gift sets~~
- ~~matching sets~~
- baby shoes

BATHING

- bathtub
- 6-8 towels
- shampoo & body wash
- baby lotions & moisturizers
- grooming kits (brush, nail clippers)
- bath accessories
- bath toys
- washcloths
- bath robes
- dental care

SAFETY

- monitor
- thermometer
- first aid kit
- ~~humidifier~~ *maybe*
- ~~purifier~~ *just don't sneeze*
- ~~gates~~ *can't move yet*
- outlet covers & plugs
- cabinet locks & straps
- car & travel safety
- kitchen & bath safety
- fire & home safety
- home first-aid kit
- aspirators

THE TWIN VERSION

We had a singleton first. That's what they call one normal baby. You won't find this out unless you're having twins. You'll think you're just having a baby, but it's really a singleton.

When we discovered my wife was pregnant again, we figured we were set. We still had all the crap from the first baby. We had kept the crib, the swing, the car seat and even a good deal of his clothes. Then we heard the "t" word. And we said the "f" word.

Twice the babies, twice the crap, right?

Thankfully, that's not the case. First off, you don't need two nurseries. You don't even really need two cribs to start. Remember these kids have shared close quarters since the day they were. They may even get a little freaked out if they can't poke each other. As they get older they'll need their own cribs, but it is not an immediate need.

The same goes for the pack'n'play—kind of a play pen mixed with a portable crib.

You're not going to need two kinds of diapers even if you've got one of each gender; at the infant stage a diaper is a diaper. They aren't specifically designed to catch boy or girl crap until they hit the toddler stage.

Do you really think you'll need two swings? Hell, yes. Do not skimp on the swings. We tried. We were foolish. Don't be like us.

You will need twice the bottles, but one bottle warmer will do.

A few months after they're born, you will need two high chairs but you should go with the ones that attach to normal people chairs. Two self-standing high chairs take up too much room. And you won't have much, because you'll have two swings and a pack'n play taking up the living room.

Here's what you'll need two of:

- *Crib and bedding (eventually)*
- *Crib mobiles (unless you don't like one of the babies)*
- *Car seats*
- *One double stroller–Get the tandem kind or you'll start to hate doors*
- *Umbrella strollers*
- *Twice the bottles*
- *High chairs (eventually)*
- *Twice the diapers and wipes*
- *Swings*
- *Twice the clothes*

Everything else you can get away with what you would get for a single child. Don't get me wrong. It's still a lot of crap to buy.

But the good news is you can sell most of your furniture and any fun stuff you have because you won't be sitting down to do anything again for three years or so.

WHAT'S NOT ON THE LIST

The list is full of crap you don't really need. But, there are surprisingly a couple of things missing.

A Small Phillips Head Screwdriver

Apparently the greatest threat to an infant's life outside of cats is that he or she will suddenly learn to crawl, open a battery cover and ingest the Energizers inside. A neat trick for a newborn really. Now, I've never seen or heard of it happening but it must have happened a ton in the 70s and 80s.

It is because of this fear that some government agency decided that all things battery powered should be sealed shut with an impossibly small Phillip's head screw.

Children run on batteries. Big D cells. And C cells. Quick

quiz, what else runs on C and D cell batteries, and you can't say flashlight? That's right. Nothing. The entire comically oversized battery division is kept afloat solely by baby crap.

And they die quickly. You don't know this yet but it is exponentially harder to find something when a baby is crying. Be prepared.

And, that is why you need one, maybe more, of these screwdrivers handy. It could be the most important tool in your house. Keep it in what will soon be called your battery drawer. I give them out as gifts to new dads. They look at me funny but come to thank me later.

A Knife

You're a father. You need a knife.

Annoying tags. Threads on clothes. Those wires that hold toys into their packages. Fighting off bears. Turning water bottles into sippy cups. Making good on threats to pop that damn balloon. Cutting things. You're going to need a knife.

Nothing ridiculous. I'm not talking about strapping a machete to your leg and scaring the neighbors. Just a simple pocketknife will get you through the day and out of most scrapes. The Swiss Army Knife is the definitive pocketknife. Several tools. Compact size. You probably got one for graduation or something. They are everywhere and they suck. Try to pry with it and you end up with a bent knife. Try to fight a bear with it and you'll cut your own thumb off. And you're not going to win a fight with a bear with just one thumb.

Sure, there're a lot of tools on it, but, face it, now that you're a parent you're not going to need that corkscrew to open a bottle of wine as much as you'll need a real blade to cut through the zip ties holding "the dolly that pees" in its Fort Knox packaging.

So, let go of your Wenger and get a single-blade folder with locking liner.

They're not bulky, so they fit nicely in your pocket. (Note: don't clip it to your belt. Don't be that guy. We all laugh at you. Twice as hard if you've got your cell phone in a holster as well, cowboy.)

It has an assisted opening so it opens quickly with one hand—good for bears that surprise you. And, trust me, if you're ever in a bear fight, it's a surprise. They are notoriously bad about calling ahead.

I prefer a partially serrated edge. The fine edge will cut a page out of a book, but the serrations will saw through rope or balloon ribbon as if either was balloon ribbon.

And, most importantly, it has a good, solid blade that has not bent on me yet.

But, that's me. There are many good tools out there. And, as long as you spend more than thirty bucks and it's not a knife from the movie—any movie—you'll be in good shape.

I think that as a father it's important to be prepared and a knife is the simplest, most versatile tool in the world. Its practical applications are endless. But, if you need one more, remember that no young boy looks cooler than the one whose dad pulled out the knife in front of his friends and saved the birthday party, fixed the toy or killed the bear.

NAMING YOUR CHILD

As you get closer to the birth of your child, the topic of a name will come up. Your kid is going to need a name because there is going to be a lot of paperwork before you leave the hospital and almost every form has a name blank on it. Hopefully, you will come to an agreement without a fight and you pick a name that suits the child.

A lot of people are going to have opinions about the name. They'll say you need to pick a traditional name. Or they'll want you to pick a more contemporary name. Some people like naming living beings after cities. Others seem to put absolutely no thought into the naming process at all. Other will try to get you to name the kid after them. Many will remind you to make sure that whatever name you choose is free of offensive playground rhymes. This is good advice but you have to keep in mind that kids can rhyme almost any name except Orange. And if you name your kid Orange, it's not really going to stop the teasing. Don't forget to double-check the initials. Veronica Alice Grayson and Craig Oliver Knight are going to get just as much teasing as Bart Fart.

When it comes right down to it, the only important thing is that you name the child what you want. And even that doesn't really matter because regardless of what you name them, they won't listen. Ever.

THE TWIN VERSION

Some people look upon the birth of twins as a gift to their insipid sense of cuteness. Just know this, if you make their names rhyme, so help me, I will find you and punch the stupid out of you. These are children, not a 1920's Vaudeville act. They will grow into adults and be forced to tell people their names. And, it will inevitably come out that they have a twin with a rhyming name. People will laugh—if not to their faces then certainly behind their backs. And they will be right to. Why would you do that to your children? I thought you loved them.

THE NURSERY

You've no doubt heard of how your wife will go into a nesting phase where she will go crazy cleaning, organizing and preparing the house for the baby. Next to having a designated driver for nine months, nesting is the best perk of pregnancy that isn't sensitive to the touch.

That is unless she's on bed rest. She'll still want the place cleaned and organized, but will have a note from the doctor saying that you have to do it. The only thing you can do at this point is play dead. But, even that might not stop her from making you work.

No matter who's doing the heavy lifting, the focus of this effort will be the nursery. There is a great deal of comfort gained from having the baby's room ready to go before the kid arrives, so it's worth your effort.

First you'll have to choose a theme. I checked and

apparently "bedroom" is not a theme. There seems to be only three options in the world of nursery decor: blue, pink and safari. Now, I'm never one to knock any idea where monkeys are involved, but I wasn't ready to give in to what was available at the store. My thoughts are, if you're going to paint anyway, might as well make it a rocket ship.

I dreamt up the idea of turning our son's room into the cabin of a retro style rocket ship and somehow sold it to my wife. I was picturing rivets and portholes. The diaper table would sit beneath a giant stencil denoting the area as the Pampering Or Odor Prevention (P.O.O.P.) Bay 1. The crib would no doubt be a Cryonic Rest and Incubation Bed and the diaper pail would be a Super Heated Incineration Treatment tube.

Star fields and planets would surround him. My tiny space cadet would dream of adventures beyond the stars. Even in his infant years he would grow a powerful imagination that would serve him well as he grew.

In the end the room was blue.

Rivets aren't easy to install in drywall and outer space has a butt-load of stars. Painting them would have taken forever.

There're a lot of things you have to do when you're getting ready for a kid. So, unless you can outsource a muralist and set designer, I'd say go with the safari theme. At least there'll be monkeys.

THE TWIN VERSION

Two boys? Easy. Two girls? Sweet. One of each? You poor bastard. Interior design shows and paint commercials have made it all too clear that you can design a single room for a boy and a girl. They'll paint a perfect seam down the middle of the room where two entirely different colors meet. Fabrics and drapes differ but complement one another as the two halves of the room are united in one picturesque setting.

The truth is you'll barely be able to fit two cribs in the room. But these shows make it look easy. So guess what you'll be doing. That's right, it's time to get out the straight edge.

If you can gain anything from this makeover at all, I suggest you show up to work with blue and pink paint splattered on your skin. No one will say anything, but the message is clear—this poor guy deserves our pity.

BRAXTON HICKS

Braxton Hicks was a probably a bastard. I hate research so I haven't really looked into it, but the contractions named after him are the false alarm of pregnancy. They send you into a panic and offer no reward for action. So, Braxton Hicks, while possessing a name better suited for a brake caliper, navy rail gun system or off-brand athletic wear, chose to attach his name to false labor. What a bastard.

These contractions are nothing to worry about, but what do you know? You've never had a baby before. But, you have heard all these stories about contractions, so when your wife feels contractions, you would assume that she's having a baby. Braxton Hicks make you worry because you don't know any better. They play on your ignorance like a total bastard.

You're wife will tell you that she's having contractions, so you pile into the car with her and all of the luggage that goes with and leave tire marks in the street getting her to the hospital as fast as physics will allow because you don't want her water to break in your car.

You rush into the hospital, where absolutely no one is freaking out, and explain that your wife is having a baby. Then, no one freaks out and they tell you fill out some paperwork. You check her in and wait a bit. The contractions keep coming. You're panicking less about her water breaking and more about why no one is panicking.

They finally take her back into a room and check her out. Soon they calmly explain to you that you are an idiot and that these are Braxton Hicks contractions and are nothing to worry about; they're perfectly normal and everybody knows that. They do not talk down to your wife.

So now you feel like an idiot. You don't like feeling that way so you decide to treat all future contractions as if they were Braxton Hicks. This is a solid plan.

When your wife does go into labor, you'll tell her that it's probably Braxton Hicks and there's no need to panic. But, now she now knows the difference and you're not only an idiot but you're an insensitive idiot for not believing her and for questioning her contraction analytical skills. Soon you're on your way to hospital with a pissed off wife.

So, I ask you, aside from the Boy Who Cried Wolf, who would want their name attached to the fire drill of childbirth? A mean old bastard, that's who. Braxton Hicks was that bastard.

Note: Though he is credited with discovering Braxton Hicks contractions, your wife will insist that women probably knew about them way before he did. Don't argue. Let it go.

YOU'RE CUT OFF

Things are going to get good when you're wife is expecting. Somewhere between the morning sickness and when the baby is using her bladder as a punching bag, there is a wonderful period of big boobs and just right hormones that will put her in a mood you haven't seen since your honeymoon.

The problem with this amazing time is that you quickly trick yourself into thinking it will last. It doesn't.

You knew this day was coming. Now instead of her headache barring you from happy time, it's doctor's orders. That's right. You will reach a point in the pregnancy where medical science is actually cock-blocking you. Sorry, champ.

The news is easier to take if your wife's doctor is a dude. He wouldn't lie to you about something like this. If your wife's doctor is a lady, however, you will probably suffer a little distrust and wish that you had gone to every single appointment just in case there was a secret conversation between the two. "Just let me know when you want him to leave you alone and I'll write you a note," says the doctor. I can totally see them doing that.

As your kid develops and your wife's stomach grows, things are going to get sensitive and uncomfortable for her in general. You're not going to make things any better by performing your sexy dance, using your sexy voice or sneaking up on her when she's asleep. It's over.

All massages will be therapeutic and if she invites you into the shower it's because she can't reach something. Now is the time to focus on her without any ulterior motives.

If it makes you feel any better, you will be earning "points" for all the unselfish attention she's getting from you. Don't rush to redeem these but know that they're there.

I have no doubt you're a clever guy, but I must warn you that saying, "Your mouth's not having a baby," while true, is a bad, bad, bad idea. Bad idea.

THE TWIN VERSION

As you can imagine, since there are two babies, you'll be not having twice as much sex. Twins are often automatically put into the high-risk pregnancy category and you're wife may end up on bed rest before the normal cut off date.

You're probably thinking that as long as she's in bed ... but, no, it doesn't work that way. You still have to leave her alone for the sake of the kids.

It's just as well. You've got twins on the way. You should practice not having sex now so you can get use to it.

PACKING FOR THE HOSPITAL

What did our mothers tell us about going out in the cold? If you stay out in the cold, you'll get sick. This is why I'm pretty sure that people who run hospitals never had mothers. The nightly room rate is what tells me they've never stayed at a hotel.

Contrary to what our mothers told us, we grew up to learn that cold environments prevent the spread of germs by interrupting cellular mitosis. Now, I may be getting my high school biology mixed up with a scene in Jurassic Park, but the point is that the hospital is going to be freaking cold.

There's no thermostat in the room so the only thing you can do is pack a sweater or two. Yes, even in the summer. In Texas. And a blanket. It may seem like overkill, but there is good reason. You remember how you ceased to exist in the eyes of the doctor?

Well, that all changes when you check into the hospital. They are a very aware of your presence. And they're trying to kill you.

It won't be obvious. No one is going to try and smother you in your sleep, poison your food or drug you when you're wandering the halls looking for a nurse to get your wife some ice chips. It's much more insidious. It's the bed.

Bed is a loose definition. It could be a cot or a recliner that turns into a sleeping area. But regardless of what it looks like it should be added to the host of weapons in Clue. It will try to murder you slowly in your sleep.

Having a child is not supposed to be a restful event. I understand that. You're not supposed to sleep through the delivery but in between check-in and go time they tell you to get as much rest as you can. Listen closely when the nurse tells you this. If she's new, you will probably hear her laugh a little or perhaps try to hide a smile because she knows that with the bed they provide you, rest would be a miracle.

Maybe murder is harsh. There is a theory that the uncomfortable bed is to prepare you for never getting a restful night's sleep again. Logically, however, it makes more sense that they are trying to ruin your back so you have to eventually return for back surgery. It's an ingenious way to supply themselves a customer base.

The extra blanket may not save your back, but if you lay it across the "mattress" it may prevent you from getting treated for puncture wounds caused by the springs.

Of course pack a charger for your phone. Once you're child is born, you're going to be using it a lot and you'd surprised how fast a three-day session of Angry Birds can drain a phone. Oh, and you'll want to call people when the kid gets there.

Pack a book so you can read ... okay, I can't even type that without laughing. There'll be no distractions for you. If you're any kind of man, you will be at your wife's beck and call for the next few days. Every time she sleeps, you should do the same.

Pack your toiletries and a change of clothes for each day you'll be at the hospital. You're going to get stinky.

HONEY, IT'S TIME

Well then, get her to hospital, Andretti. Stay safe and try to keep the car on all four wheels. If you come across a bail of hay, dry creek bed or dropped loading ramp, do not try to jump it, the resulting awesomeness will not save you any time at all.

Things may seem urgent but there will be plenty of time to get her there and get her checked in. So keep your eyes on the road and try to ignore all the names that she's calling you.

Once you get to the hospital, no one will be panicking. They'll check her in, hook her up to a ton of machines and start the long process of waiting.

SOME THINGS HOSPITALS DON'T LIKE YOU TO DO

There's going to be some downtime both before and after the kid gets there. Here are some things you cannot do to entertain yourself:

- *Wheelchair races*

- *Standing at the nursery window and asking doting new dads why their babies don't look like them*

- *Squirt gun fights with IV bags*

- *Calling dibs on personal effects in the ICU*

- *Gurney races*

- *Disconnecting anything*

- *Recreating scenes from Pigs in Space because you couldn't remember the hospital sketches they did*

- *Gender-guessing new arrivals*

- *Playing a quick game of "Who's Terminal" in the cancer wing*

- *Teasing male nurses*

- *Wearing a bedpan as a hat and delivering the Gettysburg address in the waiting room*

- *Making jokes*

- *Needle darts*

- *Playing "What's the blood pressure of everything?"*

- *Giving new babies nicknames in front of their families*

- *Bassinet races. Any kind of races really. Nothing is supposed to happen fast in a hospital*

- *Having any fun at all*

You can, however, visit the gift shop. Yay.

DELIVERY—NATURAL

You are no doubt aware that kids come into this world in one of two ways: the good old-fashion vaginal way and C-sections.

First I'd like to talk about the traditional, non-cutty way. If your wife is delivering vaginally, then DO NOT LOOK AT THE VAGINA! I told you before that there is no crisp and sterile sheet to separate you from the carnage that is childbirth. So, you, like me, pictured yourself way up at the top of the bed holding your wife's hand, stroking her hair and whispering reassuring words that you have no business whispering. That's because you're dumb, like me.

They had me right in there!

"Here, hook her knee in your arm and help hold her leg back," the doctor says.

I'm stupid so I listen. You know why she wanted me to hold it? Because it was friggin' kicking like you wouldn't believe. My wife had an epidural so she couldn't feel her legs, but the magic of the drugs also gave her the equivalent strength of a cybernetic kangaroo. She would kick and I would go flying towards the end of the table. There you come face to face with all the things you never wanted to know the vagina was capable of.

So you look at the doctor to apologize for not holding the leg back and yell at her for not warning you about your wife's augmented strength. That's when you notice that the doctor is wearing a face mask. We're not talking a catcher's mask here. We're talking a clear blast shield that covers her features from the tip of her head to well below her chin. Why is she wearing this face shield? Because, holy high velocity jet-stream of shit, blood and goo, that's why.

You spent your whole life trying to get a peek up a skirt and now you're nose to baby's emerging nose with how it can turn on you. They say that the birth of a child is a wonderful and beautiful thing, and they are full of shit. It is a wonderful thing but there is nothing beautiful about it. It's icky, nasty and makes you wince at your favorite thing in the whole wide world.

I'm not going to lie. There are going to be some trust issues in your future if you see all this. Not with your wife. Not with the doctor. Not with your child. But after seeing what's it capable of, you will approach the vagina with caution. Spare yourself this mistrust and do not look. Maintain eye contact with your wife at all times.

Also, do not let your wife hold your left hand. Give her your right to squeeze or she will use her super baby scream strength to break your fingers while using your wedding ring for leverage. I was lucky. The metal gave before my bones. I had to have the ring reshaped after the delivery.

You're going to get yelled at a lot during the delivery. Just be prepared for that. Your wife may yell at you for getting her pregnant or for doing what the doctor is telling you to do.

The doctor will yell at you for not holding back the leg/keeping your face out of all the vagina and for not knowing anything about delivering babies. I know, I know, I thought it was the doctor's job to know all that, too. They spent their post-graduate years studying and practicing it and you spent an afternoon in a classroom squirting "milk" (really water) onto the back of your hand and then trying to determine if it was warm or not. So, I can see how they would assume you've got the knowledge and skills to perform surgery.

If you're standing where the doctor told you to, the nurses will yell at you for being in the way. With all of this insanity going on it's really no surprise babies come out screaming. It's probably something you did.

There is good news though. You may not notice during all the yelling but you exist again. It's been a while, but all of sudden you are a person with thoughts and opinions. And you should be, you and the doctor are the first people on earth to see your child, and since the doctor's face shield is covered with a mixture of fecal matter and amniotic fluid, you are really the only one with a clear view of your baby.

The doctor will look right at you. Then they'll ask if you want to cut the cord. So, here's the doctor, who ignored you for months, asking you to be a doctor again. That's quite a step up from not existing. It still surprises me. I didn't go to school for doctoring, but all of a sudden they want me to wield blades dangerously close to my kid. But I wasn't having any of it. What if I screw up and the kid ends up with an outie? I'd have to live with that shame. That's a lot of pressure for someone with an arts degree. Cut the cord if you want to, but I figured it's the least they could do for what I'm paying in fees.

After the cord is cut, if all is well, they'll hand you the kid all screaming and covered in everything that didn't end up in the doc's face.

There will be tears of joy, proclamations of love, if it's a girl, you'll promise to get her a pony and then they'll take the kid to wash up the mess. You'll kiss your wife and the doctor will tell you to go tell everyone in the waiting room the great news.

This is kind of a trick and kind of not. They really do want you to share the news but they also want you out of the room for the afterbirth. What's that? Yeah, they never really covered it in baby class. The afterbirth is the placenta. If you want to think of it romantically think of it as the vehicle of life that brought your child into the world. If you happen to see, you'll know it is more like a beached jellyfish mixed with nightmare fuel that special effects artists use for inspiration to build creatures that make moviegoers throw up. DO NOT LOOK AT THE AFTERBIRTH!

Focus on the baby. It's much cuter now that they've wiped the goo off.

DELIVERY—C-SECTION

If you've planned, or end up having, a C-section, things work a lot differently.

First of all, there's a sheet! A glorious sheet lifted high and wide so you don't have to see what's going on. They put it there so you don't see them gut your wife, as if that is any more traumatizing than the eruption of the birth canal.

During the C-section, it is much closer to what we've been taught by television. You sit with your wife, staring lovingly into her eyes as your child is delivered. You hold her hand. You stroke her hair. You whisper loving and encouraging words to her as they cut her open.

All the magic happens behind the sheet and then they present your child to you without you having to see a thing.

That is unless the sheet falls down. Based on personal experience, this only happens 100% of the time. Modern medicine has invested billions, perhaps trillions, into developing new medicines, techniques and equipment that perform everything short of miracles. Surgeons can now perform procedures from the other side of the planet using remote controlled instruments. But clamps … they haven't got quite got those figured out yet.

Should the sheet fall, you will see everything. Where they cut her. Blood everywhere. What you think is blood but is really an antiseptic called Betadine, but you don't know that until later so you think it's blood therefore it might as well be blood. You'll also finally be able to identify the smell in the room as burning flesh.

Then you'll see the doctor reach right into your wife's womb like some graphic magician and pull out your child in a pool of blood.

It can look pretty nasty but, all in all, it's not as gross as the whole vagina thing.

THE TWIN VERSION

With twins the doctor will most likely suggest or insist on a C-section. The process is no different or less disgusting. The doctor will just pull out two kids instead of one. Separately. One at a time—not one in each hand like some kind of Globetrotter palming basketballs.

Seeing your first child will still be the biggest moment of your life but there is only about a minute to admire him or her before you have to split your attention to the other one. From this moment on your life will be a constant struggle to not favor one over the other.

But something else has happened here. You've not only been blessed with two wonderful children, you've been awarded the ultimate one-up. From here on out, unless they have triplets, you don't have to listen to anyone bitch about their kids ever again.

You've been given license to end all complaints with one simple phrase. And you'll need it because most of your friends are probably having kids about this time as well. Whenever they start to complain about anything baby related, just look them in the eye and say, "I'm sorry. Is your ONE baby causing you problems?" Instant silence.

This will work forever. Toddler, pre-schooler, kindergartner, teenager—never again will you have to listen to anyone gripe about the difficulties of raising a child.

Warning: Don't do this if they are talking about health issues. Then you're just being an insensitive dick, you dick.

THEY'RE WATCHING YOU

Congratulations, you are now a father—something that you know nothing about. Sure you went to baby class that afternoon and you read a few books, but everything you've learned will suddenly leave your head and a little panic may set in. Can you even remember how to hold a baby? What do you do if it cries? Is the name you picked really fitting? What if you do something wrong and somebody sees? Will they take the baby back? What the hell are you even doing there? Is it getting hotter? Was the room always this small? If you had to make a run for it, would you fit down the laundry chute? Where does the laundry chute go? Would everything be covered in old person pee? Could you hold your breath long enough?

Don't worry. All of these thoughts are perfectly normal, probably. You just had a kid. Everything just changed. No one expects you to know everything. I mean, don't drop the kid, but people are there to help you through it all. It's not like they're watching your every move. It's your kid. They trust you. Okay?

So, your kid will come back to the room with an RFID tag that looks like it belongs on a pair of jeans. This is just so they can track the baby's every move and ensure its safety from everyone that dare come near it. You know? Just to ensure no irresponsible person that knows nothing about babies ever picks it up.

Well before the baby's birth, you'll take a hospital tour. On that tour they will emphasize security in the maternity ward. They are usually more proud of this than they are their ability to bring life into the world. This security will include a system that tracks the babies so they can't leave the building without the proper parents. It's kind of like a coat check for infants.

When they bring the baby back to you, the device is installed. That's what the ankle bracelet is for. So, don't worry, your baby didn't do anything wrong, it's just a version of Baby Lojack.

I know what you're thinking here. Lojack would make an awesome name for a boy. Well, I've got dibs so you can forget about it.

MILESTONES: YOUR BABY'S FIRST CRAP

From here on out everything is about milestones in your child's development. And the very first milestone your little one will achieve is his or her first crap.

How big a deal could this possibly be? This crap even has its own name—they call it meconium.

It may seem strange to give a unique name to one particular turd but it will all make sense when you finally see this thing. This is no ordinary crap. It's black. It's not brown or green; it's black like tar. A black so deep that it drains the surrounding room of all light, drawing it in and swallowing it whole. Black like a soulless creature of forgotten lore from which, I can only assume, it draws its name. Meconium.

Meconium is not, by nature, evil. It is just a crap. But its emergence signifies something much worse. You see, it works like a plug and it was holding back all future craps. Little craps, monster squats— every turd your child will ever produce is unleashed into this world when the meconium first makes itself known.

But a lifetime of fecal production is not the worst thing that meconium produces. There is something much, much worse. That is meconium humor.

Clever minds in the button industry have made the realization that meconium means shit. And since it does, you can replace the word shit with meconium and a phrase would go from being crass to clever. And thus the phrase "Meconium Happens" was unleashed like a walled-up lifetime of crap into this world.

"Meconium Happens" appears on buttons, stickers, desk plaques, coffee mugs, T-shirts and every trinket possible. Everywhere you turn in the hospital nursery, you're going to run into "meconium happens." Even the nurses will put on their best tour guide smile and tell you that meconium happens.

I'm not sure how things work in the button industry, but it appears that once you've written some gold like "meconium happens" you can rest on your laurels and count your money because no other shit/meconium lines were ever explored despite a wealth of applications:

A **"Cut the meconium, we're having a baby here"** sign in place of the "quiet please" placards.

"Do I look like I give a meconium" onesies for angry looking newborns.

"No meconium, Sherlock" detective kits/pipes for babies.

"King meconium" brand diapers.

"Holy meconium! You're having a baby" balloons in the gift shop.

Honestly, I think it was all created by one lazy sack of meconium that didn't realize a terrible pun's full potential.

The best thing about your baby's first poop is that, unlike a lock of hair or their birth certificate, you are not expected to hold onto it, bronze it or keep it on file. Just let the nurse take care of it.

GOING HOME

Remember that time in college when you got hammered and chose to drive home anyway? And then that cop got behind you in traffic for the entire ride? Of course not, it never happened, wink, but that is how good a driver you will be when you're taking your child home for the first time. Except not drunk.

You will see stop signs you never knew existed. You'll find your blinker (hint: on the left of the wheel). You may even find yourself using hand turn signals just to make sure everyone knows what you're doing. You'll obey every speed limit and still feel like you're speeding. You'll check every mirror a thousand times and never be certain of what was in it.

The only thing you'll see in the mirror is your baby in its car seat.

Being a father still won't seem real at this point. That they actually let you leave the hospital with the child still confounds you. What kind of irresponsible institution would do that?

Even once you get home, the bafflement will continue. You'll walk in with the child in your arms, delivering him or her to their new home for the first time. You may even give the baby a tour of the house. After that, you won't have a clue what to do.

Do you put it in the swing? Seems a little soon. The pack and play? Already? You can't just hold it forever. There's stuff in the car that needs to be brought in. There is only one solution here. It will come to you quickly and it's a very crucial lesson: when you don't know what to do with a baby, give it to Mommy.

Congratulations, you are now a real father.

LET'S TALK ABOUT SHIT

With a certain amount of trickery, deception and disappearing, you can get out of changing most of your child's diapers while you're at the hospital. But you're not there any more. There's no fully staffed nursery to tend to your child's "movements" and "little messes."

Now that you are home with the baby, your life will revolve around poop. Color, consistency, frequency, odor—your life is now all about ass management. I'll tell you right now that the best day of a father's life is not when the child speaks your name, or walks, or gets accepted to Harvard, it's when that child wipes his or her own ass. But, that's a ways off so let's get back to managing your child's ass.

Poop is apparently very important. You're supposed to watch it closely for all sorts of things. Color matters for some reason and you will be amazed at the array of colors your child can produce. Really it's like they shit through a prism. An artist's canvas has nothing on the inside of an infant's diaper; its pallet is richer and contains much more meaning.

If your baby poops too much, that's a problem. If it doesn't poop enough, that's a problem. If its poop is too dry, it's a problem. Slimy, problem. Green, problem. It may not really seem like a big deal, you're just taking a quick glance into a diaper and verifying that everything is okay. Then you start to realize that it's a conversation topic. A topic well beyond, "Did you see that monster turd?"

Talk of poop will fill conversation with your wife. Catching up at the end of the day will be about the baby's crap. You'll get home and hug and kiss. You'll ask about each other's day. Each other's day will involve stories of crap.

They'll seem natural at first, but after a few months you'll come to the realization that you talk about poop more than you ever thought you would.

Also, don't ever get comfortable with the idea of poop always being in a diaper. It will be everywhere. You're going to want to start adjusting to the idea of having it all over your hands, clothes and face. Yes, face. I don't know how it gets there. Science doesn't know how it gets there. It just gets there. And the stupidest part is that you may not even know it. It defies all logic but you didn't have logic, you had a baby.

THE FIRST NIGHT

You're going to be exhausted. You've been in that hospital for three days or more, sleeping on that torture rack that somehow got an Underwriter's Laboratory stamp of approval. Your wife will probably be tired, too. You finally get the kid to bed and you collapse in your own. It's comfortable. It envelopes you in the crevice of the mattress you've spent years developing. You know you've only got a few hours before the baby monitor goes off and wakes you both but you're not worried about drifting off into a dream world free of nurses and beeping machines. It will happen quickly.

Then you think, how does my child know how to breathe? Nobody taught them. You probably explained how a car works to them on the drive home but you never covered breathing. They had people watching the kid at the hospital, maybe they taught the kid.

You're no longer sleepy. Now you're wide-awake listening to the baby monitor that you now realize is not loud enough to pick up breathing. Unless the kid stopped breathing. You'll tell yourself you're being stupid but you'll end up checking the kid several times just to confirm that, yes, you are stupid.

Every time you go in, the child is sleeping like a baby. You're just getting more exhausted. This is perfectly normal, but still stupid.

SLEEPING LIKE A BABY

Just a quick note on sleeping like a baby. Babies don't sleep very well. The phrase is the most ass-backward idiom ever. But, now that you have a baby you'll know that when someone tells you they slept like a baby what they really mean is that they woke up every hour or so, drooled and crapped themselves with regular frequency. And, they absolutely wet their pants.

DIAPERS

You're going to have the change diapers. Why? Because it's not 1955. Do you really want to be the villain in a Lifetime movie? And I'm talking one of the abusive spouse ones not the other kind they do where someone has cancer. Of course you don't. The fact that you bought this book is proof enough that you intend to be a good father. Of course, if it was given as a gift, someone might be trying to tell you something. So pay attention.

Diapers are a part of being a decent parent. This is your child. You share the responsibility for their existence and therefore their well-being and ass management. It's what you signed on for that romantic evening ten long months ago when you said to your wife, "The drug store's probably closed right now, I'll just pull out." You are simply going to have to help with the diapers.

Here's what you don't know; you don't want to get out of

doing the diapers. That makes me sound stupid, but I know something you don't. Diapers are currency. They're like little turd-filled tickets at Chuck E Cheese—the more you collect, the more you get.

Every one you change is a night out later on. Every time you jump in without her asking is her bragging on you to her friends. Change enough and you can earn a new purchase that's just for you.

Diapers are worth their weight in guilt. That's why you want to get in there before she does. You don't want her collecting all that guilt. You already owe her for carrying your child. I'm telling you, change the diapers and collect the points. This is a game you want to win.

And here's how you cheat: All diapers are not loaded equally. The bigger the mess the more guilt you collect. If it's more ripe, it's rare and worth more. Some will be leaky. Some will remind you of a water balloon. And then there are some that are barely a fart mark in an otherwise pleasant smelling scented diaper. These are worth next to nothing. Here are the words you need to learn in order to get the most out of every diaper, "Don't get up, Honey." Compassionate? Yes. But if she doesn't get up, she's also not going to see that almost every diaper you change is but a skid mark. Now you just need to act like each one is an abomination of nature with the odorous capacity to strip the paint from your walls.

I recommend fake gagging a lot. If you can hold your breath until you turn blue it's even better. Hold each "loaded" diaper at a distance. She'll thank you and you earn the guilt to cash in at a later time. Unless you're a totally terrible actor, it can't miss. It's like stuffing bills under the board while playing Monopoly.

Girls' diapers are easy to change. Undo the tabs. Wipe the excess away with the old diaper. Grab a baby wipe. Wipe again and re-diaper the kid.

With boys, it's no less difficult. TV, movies and lame uncles have no doubt prepared you for the fact that boys will pee on you. They say it's unavoidable, it's going to happen and, when it does, there will be a laugh track. The truth is, you're a dude and you know how your junk works. As soon as air hits their junk, they're going to want to go. Apply this knowledge and you'll be fine. Besides, if you get peed on more than once you should be required to turn in your penis.

For boys, you're using the old diaper for defensive measures. Undo the tabs and let some air in. Let the snake drain. Wipe the excess. Use some baby wipes and re-diaper the kid. Done. Not peed on. Good for you.

These instructions are for disposable diapers only. Some people may choose to use cloth diapers. You will learn to laugh at those people.

THE TWIN VERSION

Plain and simple, if you don't help your wife, your family will die in an avalanche of diapers. One person cannot keep up with dual ass management and stay ahead of the onslaught.

Like everything with twins, you'll want to change their diapers at the same time. Getting these kids on the same schedule should be the number two thing on your to do list right after "not dying from exhaustion." If one craps, check both butts. This, along with keeping them on the same feeding and sleep schedule, could be the only thing that keeps you sane.

Also, due to the cost of so many diapers, you'll be broke. Good luck.

GETTING OUT OF EVERYTHING

You may not get out of changing diapers but you can get out of everything else. That newborn little baby is a get-out-of-anything-you-don't-want-to-do-card/poop generator. You're not going to have to do anything you don't want to for at least a year.

Family gatherings, work functions, birthday parties—pretty much anything short of court appearances can be overruled by the phrase, "new baby." Sound tired when you say it and you can use it as much as you want without fear. No one has a right to call you on it. Especially no one without their own kid.

You probably never thought that this weak little child was so powerful, but it's deceptive. Embrace this power now. It will fade over time.

THE TWIN VERSION

Twice the kids. Twice the not doing anything. Enjoy it while it lasts. The free pass and the pity run out at three.

BOTTLES

At one point in your life, you probably said, "Dang, I love nipples. I mean, I really love them. I can't get enough of them and there's nothing in this world that could ever make me sick of them." And, who could blame you? Even the word nipple is fun to say. It starts deep in your soul and rolls off the tongue with a pop that puts it out into the world for all to enjoy. Say it slow. Nipple. What could ruin that?

Welcome to bottles. You've got to feed this baby constantly. They have one job at this age and that is to fill diapers. A near constant input of food is needed to generate that much crap and it's your job to supply it—all through a nipple.

It seems simple enough; put something in a bottle. Empty the bottle. Done. You and the beer companies have been doing it for years. But, this is a baby bottle so you know it's way more complicated than it needs to be.

If you're using formula, you're going to have to mix it. (Note: Yes, pre-mixed formula exists, but if you're using it you've probably hired someone to read this book for you so just stop arguing). First of all, this stuff stinks. We all know that it's going to be poo eventually, but can't we all pretend it won't by making it smell like banana or something? It seems they can make anything smell like bananas, so why not this?

Second, it mixes like a paste—a paste that will get into every crevasse of that bottle. No, bottles don't really have crevasses. Not until you put formula in them.

You'll need to heat the bottle. And, of course, you can't do that in the microwave because that would be too easy. No, you'll have to put the bottle in warm water and slowly raise the temperature like our forefathers' mothers did. This takes forever and the kid will certainly cry until the laws of thermodynamics catch up with your baby's demands.

I know. You still want to use the microwave and me saying you can't isn't a good enough reason not to. The reason you can't use the microwave is because it will obliterate all of the nutrients in the formula. Why it doesn't do this to our Hot Pockets or Patio Burritos is beyond science's grasp of fairness. You'll just have to use the hot water method.

Once the kid has emptied the bottle and spit up the food you just tried to feed it, you'll need to clean the bottle. This will require several specially designed brushes and pieces of equipment including a nipple brush. This is where you'll actually start to hate nipples. After a couple of weeks you may even state it aloud or confess it to your friends. You've got to scrub all of the formula out of the bottle and ream all of the gunk out of the nipple while burning your hands with scalding water.

Once they have been soaked, soaped and scrubbed thoroughly you'll have to steam them because even a board of pediatricians knows that you suck at washing dishes.

If your wife plans on breastfeeding you've probably figured that bottles won't be a part of your life, as she'll be keeping all the food in her boobs. Well congratulations, your deductive reasoning skills have brought you to exactly the wrong conclusion.

A woman's boobs are among the most amazing things on Earth, but they don't know when a kid is sleeping and they can't always be where the kid happens to be. Due to this lack of awareness, the boobs will continue to make breast milk even when the kid is not around. So it must be pumped and stored in bottles and little bags that cost too much and, naturally, can't be reused. These bags will eventually fill your freezer and it's important to remember that no matter how tired you are when you look in there, they are not really surprise ice cream cones.

Little frozen bags. That have to be thawed. But, not in the microwave. That kills nutrients. Better warm up the water, clever guy who thought breastfeeding would mean less work.

Honestly, if you don't let the kid get too far ahead of you, dealing with bottles really isn't the worst thing ever.

THE TWIN VERSION

Oh my God. Dealing with bottles is the worst thing ever. The sheer number of them is ridiculous. And you're constantly cleaning them. You're doing two dishwasher loads a day to stay ahead of the chaos and one of those loads is just bottles! It's amazing that you find time to dirty other dishes because at this point it seems like all you're doing is wiping ass and cleaning bottles.

And even though there are only two loads of dishes a day, it seems like you have to load it a dozen times. Why? Because you've got so many damn bottles that by the time you cram the last one in there the rest pop out like some sadistic version of that game Perfection. So you cram them back in just a little different and they pop up so you cram them in just a little different and they pop up so you cram them in just a little different and they pop up. And this never ever ends until your kids are drinking out of sippy cups. Then you repeat the process with sippy cups.

The stupidest part is that when you finally get all the bottles to fit you'll feel wonderful. After successfully moving bottles, rotating plates and closing the door, you'll get excited like you just beat the last level of Tetris. It is only at that point that you've finally conquered the bottles that you'll realize you left half a dozen out.

I've got no tips here. There is no solution. Just do your best and try not to go mad.

MAKING NOISE

This will be one of the most solid pieces of advice that I give so pay attention.

Don't be that couple.

Don't be the family that gets upset at people for calling the house when the baby is asleep. It's irrational for you to think that someone who is separated from you by a distance so great that it requires the magic of telephony to reach you would know that your kid is having his beddy time.

Don't be the family that yells at people for ringing the doorbell or gets in the neighbor's face because their dog barked and made your dog bark which woke your baby. You're just becoming the neighborhood ass that everyone hopes will move.

But, more importantly, you want those noises. You want all kinds of noises. When your baby first comes home it will sleep no matter what. Its body is busy developing or something and it needs the rest so badly that it will not wake up because Fido thought that the house was under attack or because somebody had the audacity to call and see how you were doing.

In fact, when your newborn is sleeping, you need to raise hell. Turn up that action movie in the living room. Vacuum. Start a band called the Din and play only the opening to We Will Rock You over and over again outside the nursery door.

This will get your child use to sleeping through the normal noises of everyday. Once it is a little older, it will sleep through anything and you won't have to be a jerk to everybody who calls the house unless that's who you truly are.

That's it. That's solid baby raising advice right there. Don't ignore it.

YOU'RE GOING TO DO SOMETHING STUPID AND INSENSITIVE WHILE THINKING IT'S A GOOD IDEA

It won't take long before looking at your wife makes you sad. She's gone through a lot and even more lies ahead. She's dealing with the same cluelessness and frustrations that you are. And, on top of all that, she's lactating. That's something you can't even do.

A loving husband would realize that she needs a break. A better husband would give her one. A great husband would use her break-time to pull off a Herculean cleaning effort.

You're a great husband so you tell your wife to plan a day for herself. You'll watch the kid, she just needs to get out of the house and do whatever she wants. She's going to end up wasting it shopping for baby clothes but it's her day so you can't complain.

While she's out you go into overdrive and somehow, using every last bit of energy, clean the entire house all while watching the kid. You turn the new baby impacted home from a diaper-ridden disaster into a centerfold from Better Homes and Gardens. Things are put up. Floors are vacuumed. Light bounces off of polished surfaces in a manner that would send Ansel Adams racing for his camera. You are a great husband.

You are also a dumb bastard.

When your wife comes home, all relaxed from shopping for baby clothes, she will smile and tear up. You'll be all proud of yourself because you're dumb enough to think she's crying tears of happiness.

It won't be until later that she completely breaks down. Why? Because of what you did.

She's been home with the kid every day since it was born and can barely find the energy to shower much less clean the house. She spends all day wondering if she can even handle raising a kid without going insane and you just spent an entire day showing her up.

Of course it wasn't your plan to psychologically destroy your wife. It just happened that way. So here's my advice. Never clean. It's for her benefit.

TIME FOR YOURSELF

It's easy to get wrapped up in your new responsibilities as guardian of life for your new child but it's important to take time for yourself as well. You'll find yourself insisting that your wife get out of the house and away from the smell of diapers. You need to do the same. Your new role of protector of the innocent may try to argue with this advice but you're going to need to ignore it.

If you had hobbies before you had the child, chances are you have not found time for them lately. Don't let them go. You're not betraying your family by getting away for a few hours every now and then and your sanity is going to need it.

If you haven't had your kid yet, this will seem strange. You're probably thinking that it won't be a problem. But, as guys, we all feel a sudden responsibility to always be there for our family. This is normal, but you'll drive everyone crazy if you never leave.

Don't neglect yourself. You'll turn into a jerk. And nobody likes a jerk.

ROLLING OVER AND THE RELATED HYSTERICS

Scoring the game-winning touchdown. Writing a doctoral thesis. Curing cancer. There're a lot of things your kid may do one day to gain the praise and adulation of family members, but none of then will compare to the bat-shit hysterics that will occur when your child first rolls over on their own.

People, mostly aunts and grandparents, are going to all but wet themselves when this happens, and if you ask them why, they won't be able to tell you. Maybe it's because this is the first milestone that babies reach after the whole meconium thing, but no one acted anything like this when the kid first crapped.

Just like dogs turning around before they nap or licking

themselves before they kiss you, it is an instinctual behavior ingrained in people to overreact when a baby first rolls over. It's just something everyone has done since anyone can remember, so they continue the tradition of getting all giddy for no good reason.

Just go with it, it's not the dumbest thing people do.

SMILING BACK

Tiny babies smile for a lot of reasons. Farting mostly. But, as they grow older their smiles become genuine reactions to outside stimuli. This includes everything from the dog farting to things that you do. This is a great opportunity for you. You now have an unwilling ally in the fight for being right all the time. Everyone knows that a silent smile is a sign of agreement and that any person that argues with a baby is going to look like an idiot.

I personally don't approve of baby talk or using funny voices when speaking to a child of any age. I think it's condescending and makes kids grow up stupid. This is one of the many issues I have with Elmo. But, if you're using it to manipulate a child to help make your point, I'm totally for it.

If you find yourself losing an argument, just turn to your baby and say, "He/she agrees with me. Don't they?" in your best silly voice while making a silly face. Instant agreement. Of course, anyone can turn the baby to their side of the argument by looking like a complete idiot, so you need to make sure you do it first.

IT'S BACK ON

It's time to start the music. It's time to dim the lights. It's time to get things started on your lovely wife tonight.

What? You need more? You're doctor-approved.

Go, go, go.

Just take it slow. There's a good chance you may have forgotten what you're doing.

FOCUS

For the first couple of months your child's eyes will look just like your stoner buddy's from college. Their eyes dart around the room as if they're taking everything in but in reality they can't see more than a few inches in front of their face.

Within a few months, this focus improves greatly and their ability to see everything will lead you to ask, "Is my child ready for TV?"

Yes. It is never really too young to open your child to the world of great entertainment. There is also a narrow window of opportunity to show them awesome movies before they can actually comprehend what is happening and you're forced to watch only kids programming. I still have fond memories of watching First Blood with my three-month-old. He loved it. We bonded.

As they get older it will be more difficult to pick movies that entertain you and the child. I've always found it easy to watch stuff with my boys. They've got some pretty good taste. My daughter, however, is all about princesses.

Even as a baby they will be surrounded by the princesses. And they'll grow up wanting to watch princess movies. Princess movies suck. There is no avoiding it.

Don't worry. I've done some of the legwork and found a few princess movies that don't suck. Here they are for when that day comes:

MOVIES WITH PRINCESSES THAT DON'T SUCK

STAR WARS

This is an easy one, but it gets you six hours of electronic babysitting and you've got a princess the whole time.

Then, if you're willing to expose your children to the prequels, you can pop in Episodes I-III. You'll most likely get through all of them before your daughter realizes that Padme was only a queen in the first movie. In the second two she is merely a senator. This is because the citizens of Naboo elect their queen. They elected Padme a queen at fifteen years old, which kind of makes you realize that any planet that stupid deserved to have its ass invaded by robots.

No matter what order you chose to watch them, the first few minutes of Episode IV introduces us to Princess Leah and there's your daughter's princess.

What my daughter thought: She'll watch them again with no argument.

WILLOW

You remember Willow. Trolls, brownies, human skull faceplates, wizards, witches, crossbows, swords, Val Kilmers, Billy Bartys. And they all collide in a struggle of good vs. evil. Evil wants to destroy a baby. Good is not so into the baby destroying thing.

That baby, who plays little more than the MacGuffin, is Princess Elora Danan. And, there's your daughter's princess.

What my daughter thought: She liked it but the whole skull faceplate thing may have been a little much. Also the moat monster looks more like a scrotum than you remember.

SHANGHAI NOON

Jackie Chan, a Chinese Imperial Guard travels to the Old West and uses Old West ladders to beat up on outlaws. Owen Wilson plays Owen Wilson and everyone has a good time.

And why does Jackie Chan travel to the Old West?

To save the Emperor's daughter, Princess Pei-Pei. And,

there's your daughter's princess.

What my daughter thought: If any of my kids didn't like Jackie Chan movies I'd have to start asking my wife some pretty hard questions about the fucking milkman. They loved it.

THE PRINCESS BRIDE

I get special joy in pulling this one off. Because, even though Robin Wright plays one of the most annoying characters in this movie, and even though it's called the Princess Bride, there's not a single princess in the entire movie.

She's a farmer's daughter who would have been a princess had she married what's his name. But she didn't. So she wasn't.

The rest of the movie makes up for the sham title. But my daughter never even questioned this one for a second. She was convinced she was watching a princess movie despite it centering on not quite Princess Buttercup.

What my daughter thought: She loved this one. Doesn't everyone?

SUPERMAN/BATMAN APOCALYPSE

Let me start by saying that my knowledge of DC's characters is limited. Long ago I decided to raise my kids Marvel and left anything they picked up about Superman and Flash to be explained as, that's the Flash, he's fast, or that's Superman, he's a loser. This, combined with the fact that DC seems to rewrite its characters' histories all the time, left me in the dark as much as the kids.

Anyway, in Apocalypse, Super Girl, Superman's cousin, comes to Earth. Batman wants to be mean to her, Wonder Woman wants to train her and Superman wants to shelter her. But, no one cares to ask what SG wants and there is a super powered hissy fit thrown.

Then Darkseid shows up and takes her to the planet Apocalypse, so the heroes track down a chick named Big Barda who can help them and they go there and fight lots of women with whips and someone named Granny Goodness who, I think, is supposed to be a woman, but looks manly and is voiced by Ernest Borgnine. They win and take boom tubes home and then fight Darkseid again and then it was over.

Okay, forget all the things I don't understand in that paragraph above; Batman was in it, and Batman is cool. They spend a lot of time on Wonder Woman's island with Amazonians in togas, and overall the movie was pretty entertaining.

Oh, and did I mention Wonder Woman? Princess of the Amazons? And, there's your daughter's princess.

What my daughter thought: She thought she was watching a princess movie the entire time.

VOLTRON

You remember the lions. You remember that they formed a giant robot. You remember that robot had a bad-ass sword. Do you remember Princess Allura, the ruler of the Kingdom of Altair?

No? She flew the Blue Lion, Voltron's right leg. And there's your daughter's princess.

What my daughter thought: She won't fall for this one again.

KRULL

The Beast and his army of Slayers invade the planet Krull in a black castle that is also a spaceship. Despite this amazing leap in technology, they still use swords for some reason. To defeat The Beast, the hero must first obtain the Glaive, an ancient bladed weapon with six prongs that was probably bought at a flea market or truck stop. Then he must travel, like, eight or nine places to find out where the castle is. He teams up with a Cyclops and thieves, a seer and some weird shape changer.

They ride on Fire Mares—horses that run so fast that their hooves light on fire and they can fly.

Once at the palace, he confronts The Beast and uses the Glaive, which proves ineffective. Through the power of love, he turns his hand into a flamethrower and defeats The Beast all to save Princess Lyssa. And there's your daughter's princess.

What my daughter thought: I'm just playing around here. I wouldn't show my kids this piece of crap.

SITTING UP

Congratulations, your child is now a threat to itself and others. The ability to roll over is nothing compared to the destructive capabilities of an infant that can't control its own legs.

Imagine this, you're holding your sweet and innocent child like you have a hundred times before. You're sitting down and supporting your pride and joy to make it look like they are standing and then WHAM—baby cranium to the bridge of your nose.

And the spasms don't come one at a time. Two more quick kicks of those developing legs and you're hit in the chin and eye socket. Your little baby has now beaten you up. A baby's ability to kick your ass is tremendously underestimated and they play to this. They lull you in with a false sense of chubbiness before launching like a baby shaped rocket right into your face.

This is why new parents look tired and beaten. Those rings

under their eyes aren't from a lack of sleep, it's the parental abuse barely peeking out from under the concealer. Ask them what happened and they'll dodge the question. Maybe they'll tell you that they fell down. They'll tell you everything except, "My baby beat me up," because it's embarrassing. But, it happens to the best of us.

These assaults will take place for the next few months and only become worse in both frequency and intensity. Their heads will only get harder and their legs will only get stronger, you're only hope is to predict their attacks and then hand them to a loved one.

The child has nothing against you; they are just acting upon an instinct that is placed in every child. Cave babies knew that more children meant fewer resources. Since that time, babies will do everything in their limited power to stop you from having more children. That being said ...

WATCH YOUR JUNK

Every child should come with a cup because your junk is in mortal danger from the minute they arrive. Once a baby has tried and failed to kill you using the head butt/baby rocket method, they will resort to destroying your ability to reproduce. This means constant strikes, steps and stomps to your manhood.

You may think it gets better as they grow older. That's because you believe in an inherent good nature in people. That will come to change. Man, in his natural state, is evil, and it is only through diligent parenting that any of us turn out the least bit good. You see, as kids get older, they get taller. Their fists and head are junk high. This means that the weak limbed baby stomp of infancy has become a full on running head butt to your crotch.

Also, because they're small, you don't see them coming. Every day, you're on guard for an attack, but the little buggers fly beneath radar and Kamikaze head first into every hope you had at giving them a sibling.

Watch your junk, man. There may be some upsides to not having more kids, but I'm sure it's a call you and your wife would like to make yourselves. Plus, it hurts.

THE TWIN VERSION

You might figure that since they already have a sibling that twins might go easy on your junk. Nope. Twice the kids makes them twice as desperate to make sure you never have any more. If there is an upside, it's that if you get hit in the junk by one kid and turn in pain, only to get hit in the junk by another kid, and you get the whole thing on camera, you could win America's Funniest Home Videos.

TEETHING

Never trust a teething baby. Love it. Cherish it. Dote on it. Promise to buy it a pony. But never, ever trust it.

They're not going to make it easy for you. About this time they are also sitting up and smiling at you. Then they do that cute thing where they reach out for you and coo. They smile, carefully hiding any teeth they may have cut already. You can't resist this and they know it, so you reach for your pride and joy—like an idiot.

You hug your child as you have a hundred times before. They'll smile once more and put their head on your shoulder. About this time you're hoping that your wife has the camera nearby. This is a moment you know cannot last forever, but even if it could live on in a photograph you could savor the warmth of the child's breath on your neck and the weak embrace of their tiny hands; hands that can barely grasp a rattle but still somehow manage to hold all of your future hopes and dreams.

You fall into the tiny embrace and then the kid sinks his teeth into your neck. This is pain. Pain you can't really describe. Physically it's blinding like being stabbed with a standard screwdriver by Sampson before he got his bangs trimmed. Emotionally, the pain is worse. Betrayal, treason, turned on by your own blood. A thousand emotions run through your head as your pride and joy attempts to rend the flesh from your shoulder.

You scream in pain and confusion. You begin to think your child is evil, some cannibalistic spawn of hatred and despotism. You had your suspicions when you saw the meconium—no good human being craps like that. But now, buried deep in your flesh is proof that this little child is here to kill you.

You want to push the kid away and run and hide under a pile of coats—big thick winter coats. But, don't worry, your parenting instincts will kick in and you'll realize you're not able to throw the kid down and run screaming.

You'll also realize that this monster is still attached to you. So you scream and make that hissing sound you do when you scrape your knee. You worm your way out and hold the child out of chomping distance. You tell him, "no" and then realize he doesn't understand. So now you feel stupid and you're bleeding. You promise yourself that you'll be more wary of the kid's tricks, but you'll forget by the next day.

THE TWIN VERSION

I know what you're expecting me to say. You're expecting me to tell you that, with twins, teething is twice as bad. Well, you're wrong because this is it. This is the consolation prize for having twins. Twins won't bite you nearly as much. Why? They have each other to bite.

My oldest must have sunk his teeth into me a hundred times, because he was evil and I never learned. Between the twins I was bitten a grand total of once.

Just sit back and enjoy it. And, don't worry, it's okay to smile a little every time they bite each other; this is God's way of saying, "Sorry bout the whole two baby thing, man."

IS YOUR CHILD EVIL?

Your baby's desire to consume human flesh will neither be the first nor last time you'll ask yourself if maybe your child is evil. All throughout their development there will be many times that it seems that your child was born without the "goodness" gene. There will be expressions, noises and poops that make you think your child could grow to lead a legion of the damned against the forces of good. This is normal.

The truth is they're just experimenting. You've gotten a grasp on how to work your facial muscles work as evidenced by your awesome gorilla impression. Babies are still working it out. They're bound to end up with some fairly creepy looks from time to time.

The smiles are the most concerning. No child should look like a deranged hotel caretaker, but they can pull it off with surprising accuracy. My oldest also chose to practice a guttural wheeze at the same time. Scared the hell out of me.

It's going to happen. Babies simply are not evil. Toddlers can be, but your kid is still a baby and any nightmares they give you are completely unintentional at this point.

BABY PROOFING

Once the kid starts crawling, your strategy will become about containment and safety. This is also where things go from mildly obsessive to completely insane.

The baby companies have figured out the most horrific way every single item in your home can kill or maim your child. They then take this idea and illustrate it in simple line drawings to terrify you into buying a device that will prevent the illustrated death.

Don't get me wrong. You've got to get the cabinet latches to keep them out of the cleaning supplies. You've got to get the outlet covers to keep their fingers out of the electricity. But, do you really need the toilet seat lock?

Baby manufacturers make it very easy for you to go overboard here.

When couples buy into all of the fear, their home becomes baby Alcatraz and appears more like a soft-sided fortress than a loving environment. Imagine a living room blocked off with baby gates. The fireplace has been sealed up with cardboard. The mantle and all tables have been lined with foam pads. Once you leave the living room, every door has a latch that prevents most adults from opening it. If the baby should somehow escape this perimeter and try to swim out through the toilet drain, they will find the seat barricaded by a spring-loaded arm.

Seriously, these defenses could stop zombies. It's your call on how much security you're comfortable with, but I will caution you that if you've got a friend over and you're having a few drinks and they can't work the toilet latch, they might just pee in your sink. And no one would blame them.

MOBILITY

We've already covered how we, as new parents, are idiots. This is never better expressed than in our desire to have our babies learn to crawl or take their first steps. That's because we don't know any better. We think it's beneficial for children to be mobile. What we don't realize is that it means we never get to sit down again.

They start by dragging themselves across the floor with only their arms. What are they moving towards? Power cords, sleeping pets and anything of value that sits on the floor. Here you'll find yourself getting up every few minutes to drag them back to their starting point and pointing them in a different direction.

From there they will turn around and go right back to where you didn't want them to begin with. It will be faster this time. You'll repeat this process a few times before you finally get the good sense to just place whatever they were after out of reach.

Once they get their legs involved it's just over. They're twice as fast and can get into trouble in the time it takes you to find the remote.

You think maybe that you'll just hold them because you forgot about the baby head butt and how, at this point, they can squirm their way out of any grasp. Just get used to getting up and down.

Once they start walking, it only gets worse. Being vertical, they can reach more things and have added the element of tripping to your list of fears. Honestly it would be best if you just sell all of your furniture. You'll never use it and they'll just find a way to either hurt themselves on it or ruin it for everyone.

With your first child, you'll have the camera with you at all times, hoping to capture their first steps for posterity. And, based on anecdotal research, everyone films the actual first steps or completely lies and tells everyone they were the actual first steps. By the time your second child comes along you'll be praying that it takes them longer to walk than the first. You may even considering greasing the floor, accidentally spilling your marble collection or laying down trip wires.

There's no stopping it. Just look at the whole experience as cardio. You could probably save some money by canceling the gym membership for a couple of years.

LET'S TALK ABOUT SHIT, AGAIN

By this point you'll have come to grips with poop. You won't wince when it reveals itself in a particularly bad diaper. If it gets on your fingers, you'll wipe it off. If it oozes down your pants, you'll get new pants. Living with poop has become second nature by now. You've grown accustomed. Complacent. That's just what the poop is counting on.

As soon as you underestimate poop, it turns on you.

I don't want this to happen to you so just I'm going to ask you to imagine entering into the nursery and seeing your perfect little child. He or she has your eyes, your wife's nose, beautiful hair that smells of youth and innocence and a toothy grin that makes it feel like your heart is being embraced by a physical manifestation of tenderness. They sit in their safari animal adorned crib beneath a crappy mural someone tricked you into painting on the wall. Their arms are raised and they're cooing to be picked up by the man they admire most in the world. That's you, big guy.

Now imagine all of that covered in shit. Those eyes are underlined with crap like the child is a linebacker for a team in some fecal football league. That nose has a brown streak down it completing the war paint of poop. And that beautiful hair that smelled of hope is caked and matted with a mousse made of turd. The toothy grin is as broad as ever but the teeth are speckled brown as if the cavity creeps turned their decay ray into crap blasters. They sit in their poop stained crib beneath a mural that someone tricked you into painting that is now, literally, crappier. Their arms are raised and they're cooing to be picked up by the man they admire most in the world. That's still you, big guy.

In no class or book did it ever mention that my child might one day dig the crap out of their diaper and rub it in their hair and on the walls like some deranged Picasso. We were totally unprepared for it. The child did it overnight so we would open the door to the nursery with big smiles ready to help them greet the day and the kid just sat before us wallowing. Our baby was still in full body pajamas at the time and had managed to unzip them and still get to the diaper.

They can't be reasoned with at this age. They will merely sit there and smile at you like they did something great. Perhaps if it was finger-paint instead of finger-poop, it would be. But, the smell alone prevented us from photographing it for posterity.

Long story short, we tried several things before we finally discovered the solution. God willing you won't need to know this, but what worked for us was cutting the feet off of the pajamas and putting them on the child backwards after making more room in the collar.

The crappy art stopped but we still opened the door with apprehension every single morning. While holding our noses. Just in case.

FIRST MOMENT OF COGNITION

One of the coolest milestones of a developing child is when they can understand you. It is this glorious moment of actual interaction that gives you hope as a parent—a brief semblance of possible control over your children. You now have one more tool in your belt aside from physically stopping whatever dangerous action is transpiring.

Certainly, it's a false sense of hope, but at that first moment of cognition there is a euphoric feeling that you're doing something right.

What makes this moment even cooler is that it happens before they can speak. Which means that they can't talk back.

My first experience with this was, of course, my oldest son. He was toddling through the living room. I was sitting comfortably. Neither of us wanted to stop.

There was a piece of paper on the floor. I asked him to pick it up and put it in the trash.

And, he did it! I'm not underselling this when I say it was the coolest thing ever.

He stopped and looked at me. Picked up the trash, opened the pantry door and dropped it in the can!

I was so excited. I called my wife and told her, in every detail, what had happened.

By the time the twins came along I knew that just because a child could understand you didn't mean they would do what you say. At least not without an argument. The greatness of this moment had worn off.

So, it snuck up on me.

It may just be a father's eyes that tells me my children are smarter than most but I offer this as objective proof—my twins could tattle before they could talk.

They would toddle to me or Mommy and point at their brother or sister and start babbling.

Once again I was sitting, something I truly enjoy, and I saw the offense happen.

My youngest son pushed his twin sister. She fell all of six inches and landed on a diaper-padded rear. This, obviously, upset her. She ran to me and pointed at her brother putting forth a prosecutor's case in complete gibberish.

"I saw him," I told her. "Push him back."

A light when on. She understood me. She did not know that retaliation had been an option. A smile crossed her face; she ran back to her brother and pushed him down onto his rear. He stood up, ran to me and started complaining in toddlerese.

"You shouldn't have pushed her."

He looked defeated. He understood.

"Now go hug your sister and make up."

They did. They hugged and made up. And ever since they have understood when we talk to them. Now, whether they listen or obey, is completely different.

BAD WORDS

As cool as it is to realize that your kids are listening, it's terrifying to realize that your kids are listening. Because, now you have to watch your mouth.

I have what some would call a fucking potty mouth, so I'll tell you what I did.

I figured out that the word monkey replaced almost any swear word and was just as much fun to say.

If someone cut me off in traffic that person was a dumb monkey.

If I ran into heavy traffic, I'd declare son of a monkey.

When I wanted to demonstrate how little I cared, I would tell someone that I didn't give a monkey.

A particularly annoying person was a monkey hole, which I would invite to eat monkey and die.

Bull monkey not only showed my doubt but created visions

in my head of monkey running in Pamplona.

Brilliant. Right? Just say it. Monkey. It's satisfying and nonoffensive. Who doesn't love monkeys? That's rhetorical but I'll answer it. Evil people. Evil heartless people don't like monkeys.

My thinking was that if I replaced all the bad words in the world with monkey even if my kid did start repeating me, it would be cute. It was a sound plan.

I did not, however, foresee the great new swear words it would create. The plan went off the rails when I messed up and replaced mother with monkey instead of the bad word. I called a driver a monkey fucker. It was accidental, but very satisfying. It was the beauty of monkey combined with the visceral sensation of dropping the f-bomb.

This mistake opened up a whole new world of insults. Ass monkey. Monkey bastard. Monkey loving motherfucker.

So, needless to say, I have no helpful advice here. Just a warning: the baby is listening so watch your fucking mouth.

TALKING

Does it really matter whose name the baby says first? You'd better believe it does. Those are bragging rights right there and you want to make sure you have them. Way in the future, your child will declare that they hate you as they slam a door. At that point you can turn to your wife and remind her that the kid said your name first.

I do not endorse baby talk. I think it's condescending to children and it makes my skin crawl the same way it does when advertisers try to rap—like my skin is trying to physically leave my body so it can beat me for not running away sooner. However, there is one caveat, and that word is Dada.

Say it proudly, say it sweetly, say it often. As soon as your child tries to start sounding out words, get in there and say it with a smile. Sing it. You'd be surprised how easy it is to replace the words of Twinkle, Twinkle Little Star with Dada, Dada, Dada, da.

You need to know that your wife is doing the same thing with Mama when you aren't looking but you don't need to worry. It is easier for babies to say d's than m's. Don't tell her that. Just tell her you're awesome.

MORE THAN A FATHER

At this point, after being a baby for all of its life, your child will become a toddler. That, of course, holds its own set of surprises, but you're more than equipped to handle it because you are more than a father. You're a role model, an instructor, a coach, a confidant, a counselor, a trendsetter and a hero. You are everything to this kid and more.

When you became a father you became more than a simple parent; you were also granted extraordinary powers.

I myself now control space and time, lord over an army of elven minions and have at my disposal a factory that puts the industrial machine of WWII America to shame.

I have risen above my C average to have complete dominion over the animals to the point to which I can make ungulates slip the surly bonds of earth and dance the sky on laughter-silvered wings.

I now possess the skills of the master woodworker who carves the rocking horse, frames the dollhouse and constructs fine musical instruments.

I have the capabilities to design, code and craft complex algorithms that manifest as visual and aural entertainment.

I thrive in harsh environments that took man generations to explore and have yet to conquer.

I have mastered biology and restructured my own physiology to such extremes that I can sustain myself on milk and cookies.

I promote countless products that contribute to the financial well-being of entire economies.

I bring excitement to millions.

I make children happy.

I am Santa Claus.

You'll be Santa too and gain these powers. Well, I guess not everybody, but at the very least you'll be the Tooth Fairy. That's kind of the same thing.

THE END

You can never be fully prepared for how much a child changes your life. Everything changes: your priorities, your views, your beliefs—everything is affected when this miracle comes home.

Hopefully, I've taken some of the surprises and uncertainty out of the pregnancy and the first year. The biggest thing is to never feel alone. If you truly believe that it's you against the baby, then the baby has already won.

People have been having babies for like a hundred years now. Everyone before you has gone through the confusion, exhaustion and frustration that you now face. And they always come out smiling because kids are totally worth all the crap they put you through and all the crap they put on you and on your clothes and on your stuff and in their hair.

Totally worth it.

Good luck, Dad. If you have any questions, don't call me. My kids are older now and I'm catching up on sleep.

The fun's not over.

Visit **DumbWhiteHusband.com** and talk with other dumb white husbands. Submit your own questions to the Dumb White Husband.

Remember this always: Together we can be dumber than any one individual can be dumb alone.

Also, check out this for all the dumb white husband adventures.

The Big Book of Dumb White Husband
If you're not him, you know him.

He's challenged the grocery store. He's confronted the HOA. He's even taken on Santa himself. He doesn't usually win. These are the tales of the Dumb White Husband and they are all available here in this collected edition.

Now you can have all the Dumb White Husband stories in one dumb place.

Dumb White Husband vs. the Grocery Store - John would rather sit and watch the game, but his wife needs some things at the store. Can he complete the list and get back in time to see the end of the game?

Dumb White Husband vs. Halloween - Every Halloween, Chris has the scariest house on the block and gives out the best candy. But, this year, someone is showing him up and he'll stop at nothing to find out who.

Dumb White Husband vs. Santa - Erik has planned the perfect Christmas for his family. The plan is foolproof, bulletproof and flame retardant. Nothing can undo the hours of planning and preparation. Nothing except maybe odd-shaped packages, ill-timed fruitcakes or an errant neighborhood Santa Claus.

Dumb White Husband vs. the Tooth Fairy - Erik always has a plan and he's sure he would have figured out the whole Tooth Fairy thing eventually. But, when his three-year-old son takes a Frisbee to the mouth, he's forced to speed things up. Between neighborhood kids with big mouths and unhelpful dentists he's going to need to improvise. Will he bend to the pressure of inflation? Will he get caught in the act? And, what do you do with those teeth anyway?

Dumb White Husband for President (A novella) - There comes a time in every man's life when he must stand for the things he believes in. John doesn't believe in bagging his grass. So, when a new allergy-prone neighbor gets the HOA to require it, there's only one thing he can do - run for President of The Creeks of Sage Valley Phase II.

John, Chris and Erik put aside most of their differences to run a campaign that they hope will see John elected as President and end the meddling of the rule-loving new kid on the block. Will they succeed? It's doubtful.

Note: Previously released as Dumb White Husband for President & Other Stories.

OTHER WORKS BY THE AUTHOR

Post-Apocalyptic Nomadic Warriors:
A Duck & Cover Adventure

The post-apocalyptic world isn't that bad. Sure, there are mutants. But, for the people of New Hope, daily life isn't so much a struggle of finding food or medicine as it is trying to find a new shortstop for their kickball team.

This makes it difficult for a post-apocalyptic warrior to find work. Thankfully, an army full of killers is making its way to the peaceful town and plans to raze it to the ground. Only a fully trained post-apocalyptic-nomadic warrior can stop them.

Two have offered their services. One is invited to help. The other is sent to roam the wasteland. Did the townspeople make the right decision? Will they be saved? Did they find a shortstop? What's with all the bears?

Find out in *Post-Apocalyptic Nomadic Warriors*, a fast-paced action and adventure novel set in a horrific future that doesn't take itself too seriously.

Tortugas Rising

Action, adventure, private islands, beautiful women, rhinos, boat chases, castles, car chases, fine dining, eco-terrorists, Savage man, The Rainbow Connection, a fortune, a father, dirty limericks, and two of the worst heroes ever to get caught up in a plot that could change the world forever.

Steve Bennett never knew his father. Now he's inherited a billion dollar empire and a stake in a man-made island chain in the Gulf of Mexico. Trying to adjust to his new situation, he and his best friend, Paul Nelson, travel to the islands and soon find themselves being chased by killers, killer hippies and rhinos. They have no training. They can't trust anyone. But, they must escape and stop a plot that threatens America.

Will they succeed? Will they live? Are rhinos nocturnal? Find out in *Tortugas Rising*, an action and adventure comedy.

Horror in Honduras (The Bulletproof Adventures of Damian Stockwell)

Raised from birth to be a force for justice, Damian Stockwell has forever trained to combat the evils of the world. Blessed with the physique of a demigod and one of the world's foremost minds, he travels to globe on a quest to confront evil and punch it in the face. At his disposal is a vast fortune, an endless array of gadgets and loyal friends.

Now, one of those friends has gone missing in a Central American jungle and the only clue is the grotesque image of a demonic tribal mask.

Dam and his trusted valet Bertrand rush headlong into danger and go face-to-face with evil incarnate to save their missing friend and attempt to destroy the Horror in Honduras.

Giving The Bird:
The Indie Author's Guide to Twitter

Attention Authors:

"Get on Twitter," they said.
"You'll sell lots of books," they said.
"They can suck it," you said.
You got on Twitter and tried to sell your books, but nothing happened. You searched for readers, but just kept attracting spam.

So, what's the point?

Twitter is a powerful marketing tool for the indie author. Within its ranks are millions of readers looking for new authors and new books. But, simply broadcasting your link isn't going to get you the attention you need.

This concise guide doesn't focus on the nuts and bolts of Twitter. It will not tell you how to gain a kabillion followers. It will tell you what "they" don't – what to tweet to build your brand as an author.

This guide is about how to sell your self as a person and a brand, one tweet at a time, to an engaged group of followers.

So, why is the guide so short? Because, just like on Twitter, it doesn't take a lot of words to communicate a powerful message.

More about the author:

Benjamin Wallace was born so awesome in Carleton Place, Ontario that they placed his baby picture on the front page of both town newspapers.

After that, he wrote books. This is one of those books.
He hopes you like it.

Visit the author at benjaminwallacebooks.com
or dumbwhitehusband.com.

Also, find him on twitter @BenMWallace or on facebook.

Made in the USA
Lexington, KY
17 July 2013